THE SCHOOL THAT WENT ON STRIKE

ALSO BY PAMELA SCOBIE
A Twist of Fate

THE SCHOOL THAT WENT ON STRIKE

Pamela Scobie

Oxford University Press
Oxford Toronto Melbourne

Oxford University Press, Walton Street, Oxford OX2 6DP
Oxford New York Toronto
Delhi Bombay Calcutta Madras Karachi
Petaling Jaya Singapore Hong Kong Tokyo
Nairobi Dar es Salaam Cape Town
Melbourne Auckland

and associated companies in
Berlin Ibadan

Oxford is a trade mark of Oxford University Press

© Pamela Scobie 1991
First published 1991

A CIP catalogue record for this book is available
from the British Library

ISBN 0 19 271647 6

All rights reserved. No part of this publication may be
reproduced, stored in a retrieval system, or transmitted,
in any form or by any means, electronic, mechanical,
photocopying, recording, or otherwise without
prior warning of Oxford University Press

This book is sold subject to the condition that it shall not
by way of trade or otherwise, be lent, re-sold, hired out
or otherwise circulated without the publisher's prior consent
in any form of binding or cover other than that in which
it is published and without a similar condition including this
condition being imposed on the subsequent purchaser

Typeset by Pentacor PLC, High Wycombe, Bucks
Printed in Great Britain

To Jennet and all my teachers
- past, present, and future

CHARACTERS IN THE STORY
All children have parents unless otherwise stated, but they are only mentioned if they feature in the plot

IN SCHOOL
Annie Higdon, Headmistress of Burston Council School
Her husband Tom, Assistant Master

IN CHURCH
The Reverend Charles Eland, Rector of Burston
His wife and family

THE VILLAGE CHILDREN
Dora Watson
Alexandra Watson (Baby)

Violet Potter

Marjory Ling

Emily Wilby
Mabel Plumtree
Sabina Durbidge

Jimmy Wittle (Smelly)
Sam Todd
Billy

Gladys & Ethel, fostered by:

THE GROWNUPS
Fred Watson, Dora's Dad
Ivy Watson, Dora's stepmother
Ivy's Auntie Win

Mr & Mrs Potter
Violet's Uncle Harry, the postman

Harry Ling, Marjory's Dad
William Ling, Marjory's uncle
William is the Sexton, and married to the infants' teacher.

George Durbidge, Sabina's dad, local poacher and market trader

Mr & Mrs Philpot

THE FARMERS
Farmer Todd, Sam's father
Fisher, also one of the School Managers
Bob Ford

SMALLHOLDERS
Noah Sandy
Henry Garnham, married to Bob Ford's sister
Herbert, their son. Daisy, their daughter.
Blind Ambrose

OFFICIALS
Mr Ikin from the Norfolk Education Committee
Mr Peggram, the man from NUT
President of the Inquiry and 2 assistants
Henry Lynn, KC, Mrs Higdon's lawyer
Mr Cooper, his clerk
Mr Reeves, the Rector's lawyer
Magistrate in Diss

OTHER VILLAGE FOLK
Landlord of the Crown Inn
Mrs Boulton, the Postmistress
A ploughboy
Barney the hedger

OUTSIDERS
The gipsy woman
Captain Meyer and German Prisoners of War

OLD ENEMIES
Gamble from Wood Dalling

NEW FRIENDS
Sylvia Pankhurst, campaigner for Votes for Women

ACKNOWLEDGEMENTS

I am very grateful to the following, whose works provided invaluable material for this story:

Bertram Edwards *The Burston School Strike* (Lawrence and Wishart 1974)
Betke Zamoyska *The Burston Rebellion* (Ariel Books)
The Living Archive Project *The Burston School Strike* (Oxford University Press)
and to the NUT library for loaning me its package of documents on the strike.

Many thanks to Maurice Philpot, Secretary of the Burston Strike School, for giving me his time and expert knowledge, answering my trickiest questions and providing many useful maps and illustrations. Any errors or alterations are all my own.

Special thanks are due to Ron Heapy of Oxford University Press for initiating and guiding this project, and for his support and encouragement of its author. Without him, this book would not be here.

PART I: FIRST TERMS

I live:
For the cause that needs assistance,
For the wrong that needs resistance,
For the future in the distance,
For the good that I can do.

Lines written in the back of an account book belonging to Joseph Arch, the founder of the farm workers' unions, whom Tom Higdon visited in 1909.

CHAPTER I

He picked up the knife.

"You're in trouble now, my girl," he said softly. "No getting out of it this time."

Their eyes locked. The shaky feeling she always got inside when he looked at her Like That, started up again worse than she had ever known. She took a breath, and held it. Sweat wriggled out of her hair.

He was waiting. For her to speak, to challenge him. That was The Rule. But if the shakiness got out into her voice, she knew that she would be lost.

Her lips parted.

"Says who?" she asked, very high, very light.

Without taking away his eyes, he tested the tip of the blade against a calloused thumb.

"Says me."

They stared at each other, the big man in the chair, the small, hot-faced girl in smock and button-up boots with her back to the range. And neither of them moved. The room seemed to dissolve and tilt around her, the man's face became a blur . . . but the eyes within it never wavered, willing her, *daring* her to look away, to drop her guard, to give in.

Time dripped out of the kitchen clock.

The worst thing was trying to watch both eyes at once. Her own eyes felt as if they were rattling madly from side to side, but *his* never flickered. So she tried just watching one eye. And that was her mistake. Because just when she thought she had got the shaking under control, or at least pushed down for a moment, the eye *moved. On its own.* The right eye slid in towards the nose as if it were trying to look at the left one. And the shaking jumped up from her stomach to her shoulders. But she held on. Just. And then the *left* eye rolled across to look at the *right* one . . . and the shaking

1

shook itself out through her mouth in a single unstoppable shriek —

"Oh, Dad!"

And she ran over and climbed up him and knelt on his knees and took hold of his ears and laughed right up into his face.

"*Honestly!*"

"Careful!" he said, dropping the breadknife on to the chequered cloth and steadying her with his big hands. "Nearly cut yourself!"

She poked out her tongue at him. "You're *rotten*."

"You went first." He permitted himself a modest grin. "Knew you would. You always do."

"You *cheated*." She pulled his ears. "Where'd you learn to do that with your eyes?"

"Been practising. Took me a week to crack it."

Dear, lovely old Dad, how typical! Spending a whole week teaching himself to cross his eyes just so he could keep on winning The Game. She let go his ears and started twisting his eyebrows up into wings.

"I'll beat you one day," she promised. "You see if I don't."

"Maybe you will, girl," he said, his voice suddenly soft. "Be a sad day for me though when you do."

"Why's that?"

"Because it'll mean you've grown up. When you're too old to laugh at my jokes."

Dora considered this. It didn't really seem likely that she would ever be able to withstand any of Dad's Special Looks, which always made her feel as if she were being tickled all over inside by a dozen feather dusters. She put on a solemn face.

"I'll *always* laugh at your jokes. And you know why?" He shook his head. She crowed in triumph: "'Cos you've got a silly mug, *that's* why! Especially now." She gave his eyebrows a final tweak and leaned back to admire the effect.

He squeezed her lovingly — she wasn't too old for *that*, even if she *was* nearly half past ten and had been running the house practically single handed for months—stroked her cheek and gave her an anxious appraising look. "You spend too much time at that stove. Got a face like a toasted bun. Hot and cross."

"*Who's* cross?" She scrambled down. "And why—" She gave him her quizzing stare. "—am I in trouble? Or did you make that up?"

"No," he said levelly, quizzing back. "I didn't make it up. The new teachers are coming. So you're going to have to go back to school."

"*What* new teachers?"

He smiled and folded his arms, doing his Nosey Neighbour impersonation. "Well! Mrs Moore had it from Violet Potter's Uncle Harry, the postman, the one that lodges with them—"

"DAD!"

"They're arriving tonight. Couple of hard nuts, by all accounts so they'll want you back behind that desk double quick."

"Well, I'm not going. I'm needed here."

He went on talking as if he hadn't heard. "Mr and Mrs Kingdom, I think it was. And here's a funny thing: she's the boss. He's only assistant master. Bet she knocks the stuffing out of him when they're on their own!"

You can talk, she thought, sudden and savage. *You can talk.* He seemed to catch the thought like a whiff of burning paper, for his face creased momentarily. But he said simply, "Why's the table only laid for two?"

It had been going to be a special tea. Just her and Dad. For once. Dora bit her lip, said nothing.

"Where's Baby?" asked Dad.

"*She* took her into Diss for the afternoon."

"*She*? Who's she? The cat's mother?"

"Well she's not *mine.*" It was out before she could stop it. Pain flickered up in his eyes, then his face closed round it like a hand cupping a match. He hauled over the loaf. Lifted the breadknife again and started sawing off a doorstep.

"Sit down then, and we'll get stuck in."

She took the high stool. Dad buttered her a slice, scooped it up on the flat of the blade and slid it on to her plate.

"Go on. Eat."

He waited till she had her mouth full and then said: "You don't have to be afraid of Ivy. She can't ever take the place of your mother. You know that."

But does *Ivy*? Clever Dad. She'd have to chew and swallow before she could answer. It would give her what he called Thinking Time, so she wouldn't come out with the first daft thing that came into her head. A bad habit of hers.

"And she doesn't want to," he went on.

She chewed and thought. Tried to be fair. Tried to swallow down the anger with the bread. As if it was buttered with it. It tasted of anger. Sour and hard. "It's not that I don't like Ivy," she began. (I *hate* her, she thought.) "We just don't *need* her."

"Come on, love. Your Mum wouldn't have wanted this — you missing school, working yourself daft looking after me and Baby."

"I don't need to go to school. You can teach me. You know more than all them teachers put together."

"*Those* teachers."

"See!"

He chuckled. "You're nobody's fool! And that's why you've got to have the best. Your Mum made me promise when she — when she . . . "

He couldn't say it. Dora had a sudden vision of Mum as she was when they first came to Burston, eighteen months ago in the hot July of 1909. Brushing out her long hair in the sunshine — deep chestnut, not a hint of grey.

Dora had fair hair like her Dad's, and insisted on having it cut short because plaits got in the way of tree climbing and dropped into the soup. "It suits you," Mum used to say. "I'd do the same, but your father would never forgive me. Besides, I'm just an old Victorian at heart." But Queen Victoria was dead too, over nine years now, and her grandson George was on the throne . . .

After the funeral, Dora found the old silver backed brush, its bristles tangled up with chestnut strands. She combed them out carefully and, not knowing why really, put them away in a special place where Dad never looked.

That was the day Ivy came. She was a relative of Mum's, quite a bit younger. Dainty, pretty and as efficient as bleach, with a neat oval face like something on a cameo and impeccable black plaits wound round it, so shiny they might have been varnished. She cycled over from her aunt's house in Diss every day "to look after Fred and his poor children." Whether they liked it or not.

Dad was speaking again. "Your Mum wanted you to have a normal childhood."

"That's not true!" Dora's eyes sparked. "Nothing about us is normal. We're different. Special. You said so."

"Maybe I thought so once." She noticed he hadn't touched his own bread, just pushed it round the plate with a big blunt finger as if he couldn't decide where it should go. "Your Mum, God rest her, tried to fit in with me. But what she wanted was an ordinary husband, not a lunatic who painted pictures nobody would ever buy, who dragged her off to the country and wore her out with worry till she hadn't the strength to fight off a little fever . . ." His voice wobbled.

But she loved you! Dora wanted to shout. She wanted you to paint pictures. She didn't care where we lived. We managed. We always managed. But she was afraid, confronted with the man's grief, that the words would sound false and theatrical.

"We managed," he said, with that curious telepathy he sometimes had, as if her thoughts were so strong they printed themselves on the air and he could read them off, "with her little bit of money. I never made enough to keep us. I thought it would be cheaper here."

He looked at his hands. "What made me think I could be an artist? With paws like these? More like boxing gloves. I must have been mad."

His fingers clenched round the slice of bread. Butter squashed up between his knuckles. Embarrassed, he dropped the mangled lump back on to the plate.

"You're not to stop painting!" said Dora, frightened.

He pulled out his handkerchief and wiped his hand. Very carefully, not looking at her.

"What else can I do? There's no money left. No . . ." He lifted his head and faced her. "I've put my brushes away and they won't come out again until I've proved I can be a real provider. I messed things up for her but I won't mess them up for you. I'll work on the land. Better men than me have done the same. And you—" Their eyes locked again. "—will go back to school."

"And who'll look after Baby?" she flashed. But she didn't want to hear the answer and hurried on, hoping to forestall it. "Ivy can't keep coming backwards and forwards. We don't need her, she's got her own life to lead. *You're not to stop painting!*"

As she said it, she realized that she was trying to tell him something else, but that she didn't dare, because putting it into words would make it a reality. And then she saw with horrible clarity that this was what it was all about . . .

What a bit of luck it had seemed when Ivy suggested taking Baby out for the afternoon! (She was called Alexandra really, and was actually four.) How she'd jumped at the chance to be alone with Dad like they used to be in the old days before That Woman had arrived and started to take over. Now she saw that they had plotted it all between them and that Dad had been pretending the whole time. Because he was a coward. Because That Woman knocked the stuffing out of him when they were on their own.

Her face was wet. She was crying and hadn't noticed. And Dad was saying something to her, something about having been to Mum's grave to talk it over and that he knew it was the Right Thing. Then he was saying what she had known was coming for a long time although she'd refused to recognize it. And he was crying too, only you couldn't see the tears.

"I'm going to do it, Dora. It's for the best. For all of us, if you could only see it. I'm going to marry Ivy."

CHAPTER 2

"Tom . . . *Tom!*" A small, impertinent foot reached across the gap between two prickly red plush railway seats and nudged the worn tweed knee of the gentleman opposite. "Put down that stuffy old book. I want to talk."

"Later, dear," said the man patiently. "I'm trying to work."

"What for?"

An exasperated sigh lifted, then dropped the gentleman's moustache. "Because, little Annie, we have school first thing tomorrow morning, and we want to be well prepared."

"Why? Will we get into trouble if we're not?"

"Very probably."

"Then don't let's go! Let's jump out at the next station and change trains and run away!"

The moustache bristled. "Now you're being childish."

"What's wrong with being childish?"

"Nothing. If you're a child. But you're forty-six years old, and from tomorrow morning you'll be Headmistress of Burston Council School. So you'd better start getting used to the idea — Ow!"

The book flew up in the air as the dumpy little woman hurled herself at her companion and cuddled up chuckling in the crook of his arm. Two eyes as bright as collar studs twinkled in a round comfy cushion of a face, and a tendril of wiry grey hair sprang loose from under her sensible black hat.

"You're so *bossy*, Tom Higdon!" she reproached lovingly. "Nobody would ever guess you were five years *younger* than me, the way you carry on!"

He put his arm round her, tugging at his moustache with his free hand — a nervous habit, which meant he was deep in thought.

"You wouldn't really want to run away, would you, Annie?"

"Of course not! But I'd like to show the Norfolk Education Committee just what I think of them. *Eight years* we were at Wood Dalling, Tom, and they think they can just shunt us on down the line because we stood up for what was right."

"It was a good eight years," he nodded. "We've nothing to be ashamed of. We must have got the Managers to build nearly a whole new school by the time we were through!"

"Well, they'd better not just sit back and enjoy it. Those children and their parents have got used to having somebody to fight for them. I hope they don't give up now we're not there."

Tom sighed. "We got sacked for our efforts when you come down to it, even if they *are* calling it a transfer. Folk'll think twice before they step out of line again." He dug into his pocket and hauled out his pipe. "Know what galls me worse than anything? The thought that Gamble and his cronies think they've beaten us. I'd like to punch his smug face inside out."

"*Ahem!* You did that once already! Remember?"

"Oh, yes!" Tom grinned, gripping the pipe between strong white teeth. "Remember the headlines? *Six of the Best for School Manager! Teacher Thrashes Parent!*" He took a satisfied drag, and a cloud of sharp, sweet smoke wafted across the compartment.

"It's nothing to be proud of."

"It did me the power of good at the time!"

"Now who's being childish?"

"I thought you *liked* being childish!"

"In a different way, Tom." She wriggled away, face rumpling as she sought the right words. "If growing up means accepting things the way they are, then I won't do it! And I won't let my children do it either! The wonderful thing about children, Tom, is that they still have *hope*. Too many teachers try to knock it out of them, make them conform because it makes their own lives easier. They teach through fear because *they're* afraid, they *tell* children things, but they don't let them *ask*. Well, my pupils are going to learn how to ask questions — like how they can have better lives than their parents did, how they can get off the land if they want to, or find ways of making that work better. I'm going to teach them to square up to Authority, to the Grown-ups who think they can have it all their own way — I'm going to teach them how to *live*!"

"Steady on, steady on, old girl!" Tom grabbed her hand and squeezed it. "You're preaching to the converted, you know!"

"Yes, Tom." She squeezed back. "That's why we make such a good team. I start them off, and you keep them at it when they've left school. Between us, we'll beat the Grown-ups yet!"

"That's my girl! Whoops, look lively! I think we're arriving somewhere."

The train was slowing down. A wheezing gush of steam bulged in through the window like froth curling over a pint glass. There was an indignant screech of metal, a thump, and the couple were flung back in their seats.

"Diss!" came a hollow cry down the platform. "All change!"

"Diss?" Annie dragged off her hat and banged it against her knees to knock out the dents while Tom leaned out and hailed the guard. "I thought this train went straight through to Burston."

"Not tonight it doesn't," he said, turning back, his moustache bunching irritably under his nose. "We'll have to walk. Four miles — and it looks like snow!"

"So be it!" Annie straightened her long skirts and jumped up, clutching her brolly. "A brisk walk never killed anyone."

Tom knocked out his pipe into an empty tobacco tin, and reached down their single suitcase. Opening the carriage door, he sprang out nimbly and lifted his wife after him.

"Allow me to escort you home, my dear," he said, his good temper restored. "Wherever that might be."

Dusk was drifting down outside the station in petals of black blossom intermingled with sleety flakes. Cold, bony trees stuck up out of a flat landscape like the tails of dead cats. Pulling up their collars, then linking arms, the new Headmistress and her Assistant Master set off smartly. A little over an hour later, they waded through an icy ford and entered the village.

"Welcome to Burston!—even if it does sound like a rotten tomato!" Annie flapped her wet skirts, determinedly cheerful, although she was beginning to suspect that her feet had frozen themselves into the shape of two lace-up boots, and she was in dire need of a cup of strong tea. "Quite a pretty spot—Pink washed cottages, and a windmill!"

"Pretty to look at," grunted Tom. "A different story when you get inside, I'll bet—damp running down the walls and rats in the rafters. And not much of a welcome! No one to greet us, no fire in the grate and probably no supper. A fine beginning!"

"At least it *is* a beginning!" They smiled at each other and hurried on past a derelict carpenter's shop and over the Village Green.

"Now, then!" said Tom. "Find the church tower, and the school won't be far off!" He stared round and gave a bark of laughter. "Well, there's the church. And it hasn't *got* a tower!"

"It's an omen!" giggled Annie. "A church without a tower! Wonder what the Parson will be like—a saint without a halo? Or a shepherd without a flock?"

They soon found out.

CHAPTER 3

Dora blew out the candle and lay back in the darkness staring at the uncurtained window where muzzy snowflakes bumped the pane like the mouths of startled fishes. Baby was asleep, worn out after the excitements of the afternoon. And That Woman was still downstairs. The front door opened. Voices drifted up.

"Don't worry, Fred." (It was Ivy, being *nice* — couldn't he see through it?) "She's bound to be a bit resentful at first."

Don't you *dare* talk about me! Dora sprang off the bed and scrambled up on to the oak press where they kept the spare blankets. She squashed her face to the window and listened hard.

"You go and have a quiet drink with your friends," Ivy was saying soothingly. "I think you've earned one."

Dora was a well brought up girl, but just then, she would dearly have loved to send a great angry jet of spit right down on to those black shiny plaits. Go for a drink indeed! Bet that's the last time she lets you do that!

"As long as you're back by eight," Ivy went on. "Auntie Win's sending the pony and trap, I mustn't be late. People might talk. Even if we are . . ." the voice went soft and shy ". . . engaged."

"Yes, we are, aren't we?" Dad's voice had gone soft too, and sort of wondering. Dora fought down an urge to bang the window shut so hard that the house would fall down on the pair of them. She strained her ears furiously instead, trying to make sense of the sudden silence below. Then Ivy gave a sort of gasp and a stifled giggle, and Dad cleared his throat mumbling, "Well, I hope you don't think me too forward," and Ivy said, "Not at all, not at all," very flustered, and, "Off you go, then," in her normal firm bright voice, as if he were a schoolboy being sent on an errand.

11

Dora's cheek was pressed so hard against the pane, she could almost taste the glass. Dad was walking down the path now, leaving big footprints in the light covering of snow, and pausing with his hand on the gate, to wave back at the front door. She wanted to punch her fist through the glass and scream at him: You Stupid Idiot! I'm the one you should be waving to, not her! She doesn't care about you! He dipped his head to avoid the snarled apple branches which give their home its name — Blossom Cottage — and disappeared from sight.

Dora got back into bed and pulled the covers up over her face. She lay, rigid as a corpse, her blood congealing with fury. That's right, she said talking to him in her head. Run away. Don't face up to it. Run away. That's what you always do.

Dora's Dad gave a sigh of contentment as he stepped into the familiar treacly fug of the Crown Inn. It was like being licked all over by a big, affectionate, boozy old dog. Shaking off snowflakes, he stomped through the sawdust to the bar. One or two of the regulars grunted: "Evening, Fred," between long swallows of bathwater warm ale; the rest went on muttering dourly about the ploughing, which was behind schedule owing to the frost.

Farmers Fisher and Ford were leaning up against the counter, each with a dung-shod boot clamped on to the foot rail. Fisher, lean and snide, with a prominent Adam's apple, lowered his glass and gave Fred a mocking grin, while the big fair-haired man waited placidly for his pint to be pulled.

"Painted any good pictures lately?" he asked innocently, a thin moustache of foam wriggling derisively on his upper lip.

"Done with all that," said Fred shortly. 'Matter of fact, I came to ask if you two needed any extra help."

"Well, we don't want any murals painting on the cowshed wall!" sneered Fisher. "Don't want my Tinkerbell dropping her calf early out of fright! Drop of whitewash wouldn't go amiss though. But I suppose an *artist* wouldn't stoop to that?"

"I'll do anything — if you're serious."

At this, the other farmer, a vast, shiny man like a jellied whale in leather gaiters, belched thoughtfully into the contents of his glass. Two tiny eyes, stuck in a big pink face like raisins in a glazed ham, lifted and fixed themselves on Fred.

"Want to learn to sweat, boy?" enquired Bob Ford. And, as if offering themselves as his credentials, two fat droplets of sweat oozed out of his sausage nose and plopped on to his belly. "Farming's no joke, y'know. Ain't all maypole dancing and cream teas like you city folk seem to think."

"I've lived here over a year now," replied Fred. "And I'm not afraid of hard work. Your place tomorrow?"

The currant eyes looked him up and down.

"Well, you're a big, strong fellow . . . Five thirty sharp?"

"Fine. What kind of wages did you have in mind?"

The currants vanished down a crevasse of frowning fat.

"Afraid I didn't quite catch . . . "

"How much are you paying?" bellowed Fred, then looked round, shocked by the sound of his own voice. Everyone else in the smoke-filled room seemed suddenly to have been trapped in a sepia photo, pints arrested on the way to or from open mouths, all eyes fastened on Ford. The farmer gave a greasy chortle.

"If you can pull your weight along with these other layabouts . . . I reckon you could pick up twelve shilling and sixpence a week."

"Don't go mad," muttered Fisher. "You'll pinch half my men."

Ford pushed forward an ear as big as a gammon rasher with a podgy finger. "What you say?"

"You heard. And you'll regret hiring this one — no offence, Fred. When a man goes out of his class, it's always trouble. He looks the part, but he's had too much schooling. Your men won't want to work with a fellow who looks down his nose at them — if he lasts more than two days, that is."

There was silence in the taproom. The eyes prodded.

"Maybe I've had a better education than some," said Fred carefully. "But I hope it won't spoil me for working with decent men, any more than being born on the land should stop a good man from becoming anything he wants."

"Well said!"

The stranger in the corner, who had been sitting silent for the best part of an hour, lifted his glass in a salute.

"What's it to you?" demanded Fisher, Adam's apple joggling.

"My father was a farm labourer," replied the stranger, "but it didn't stop him being a man. That seems to be *your* mission in life, gentlemen. And good Farmer Ford here didn't grow that belly on twelve bob a week!"

Ford's belly and chins juddered with mirth. "True enough, boy!" he said. "But I didn't grow it on fancy *talk* neither. As for this lot—" He waved an arm big as an ox carcass at the listeners, whose sharp, bony faces had turned eagerly in the stranger's direction. "They know who puts the bread on their tables. And *what* puts it there—*Sweat*, boy. Not words." His curranty eyes rested for a moment on Fred. "Don't go political on me, there's a good chap. We'll get on very nicely if we know where we stand. I don't want telling what to do on me own property."

Ford lumbered to the door and paused expectantly. Somebody scurried to haul it open. The night roared in at them, a cold black furnace-mouth full of white dancing sparks. Ford's huge bulk filled up the gap as he paused on the threshold, and Fisher moved in behind to shield himself from the wind. Then the door creaked shut, and everyone in the taproom started talking at once.

"Mind if I join you?" Fred asked the stranger.

"Help yourself," said the other, stroking his moustache meditatively. "I take it those were the local bigwigs?"

"Oh, Ford's all right—the fat one." Fred settled himself on a bench and studied his companion. Obviously not a labourer—a travelling salesman of some kind maybe. "It's as well not to rub either of them up the wrong way," he

14

warned. "The farmers round here run pretty well everything. And that includes running folk out of town!"

"Oh, they're *Parish Councillors*. School Managers too?"

Fred nodded. "Fisher is. Not that there's much to manage. We've a job keeping teachers. There's only Mrs Ling at present—she takes the infants. But when Mr and Mrs Kingdom come—"

"Kingdom come?" The stranger smiled, but did not share the joke, remarking instead, "If twelve and six a week is the going rate for farm labouring, don't your unions need shaking up?"

"*Unions?*" came a voice from a nearby table. "We don't want unions round here. Calling for strikes and what have you. Can't none of us afford to be out of work."

"But a union could *help* you," the stranger tried to explain.

"Naw," said another, shaking his head. "'T would offend the Parson for us to be idle. The Bible says a man must labour."

"It also says the labourer is worthy of his hire."

"Not if it means the little 'uns get whacked at school to pay for the sins of the fathers..."

The stranger's face went very pale, like a man's does when he needs all his blood to fuel his fists. "You mean to say that the teachers would punish innocent children if their parents went on strike?" He stared round at the faces—anxious, exhausted, but lit with a strange energy like the power which lifts ghosts out of the grave—the energy of fear.

"If the Managers told 'em, they'd 'ave to," muttered one.

"Stands to reason," asserted a toothless old fellow, a hedger by trade, as twisted and scraggy as one of his own hawthorne bushes. "When folks start hooliganizing and striking, the High Ups always say it's because they wasn't schooled right. So they cracks down on the nippers before the blight spreads. That's what teachers is for—to learn them their place."

"Oh, you mean, whack them first and they won't ask questions later?" asked the stranger sardonically.

"Being whacked never done me no harm," declared the hedger. "I'm eighty three or four, and as fit as the day is long."

"And what's *that* worth?" jeered a young ploughboy. "You're in the same rented cottage you was born in, only it's eighty-four years older now and even more decrepit than you are!"

The old man rustled with indignation like a bunch of dried kindling. "I don't hold with change!" He jerked a knobbly chilblained finger at Fred and his companion. "So don't you go stirring things up — It ain't new fangly danglies as has made this country great. We didn't get us an empire by complaining!"

"What empire?" scoffed the boy. "I share a room with six brothers, and I can't get wed till my Dad dies — there's no room to put a wife!"

"Maybe the new teachers will bring some new ideas," offered the stranger. "Your children at least should have a chance to — "

There was a prolonged and startling rasp and the percussive chong! of tobacco-juice hitting the spittoon. All eyes swung in its direction. Leaning up against the chimney breast was a powerful, squarely built man with thick, crinkling black hair, brick red cheeks and a flashy yellow waistcoat. He grinned, showing several gold teeth among nicotine brown ones, and threw down his large whisky in a single gulp.

"Teachers!" he said. "Bowing and scraping to the Parson they'll be and teaching what he tells 'em or they'll be out on their ears. They're a lily livered breed. There's things they could tell our brats — about life, the world, what goes on outside of Burston — but you know something?" He thumped his chest. "George Durbidge never met a schoolmaster yet, for all his special learning, that had the guts to share it!"

With a flourish, he bent down and hefted a fat and sinisterly squelching sack on to his shoulder. "Be your own boss," he advised the company. "Don't take orders from no man, squire or farmer or priest or teacher." He looked at the stranger. "Or rabble rouser," he added. And he swung out into the night.

"All right for some," muttered the ploughboy. "Damn' poaching swine. Beats his wife and all."

At this, the stranger gave a start. "I'd better cut along," he said with a rueful grin. "Told the wife I wouldn't be long."

Fred jumped up hastily. "Is it gone eight? I'll come too." There were guffaws all round. Everyone's spirits revived.

"So much for the politicians!"

"Soon as the wife whistles, off they trot!"

The snow clouds had shifted, leaving a pale dust over the cobbles like freshly strewn ashes. Fred pulled his cap down over his ears. "Good luck, friend," he said, and turned to go.

"Let's meet again and talk," said the stranger. Fred shuffled his feet. "No offence," he murmured. "But I don't want to get into politics, just earn a living."

The stranger smiled. "As you wish. Good-night, then, Fred."

"Good-night, Mister . . . er . . . ?"

"Higdon," grinned the other. "Tom Higdon." And he strode off whistling into the darkness.

CHAPTER 4

"Well, this is it!" said Mrs Ling proudly. "Our little school! Does it meet with your approval, Madam?"

Half-past eight next morning. Annie Higdon's eyes lingered for a moment on the infant teacher's shining face, then moved reluctantly round the dingy room with its cracked panes, peeling paint and shabby desks crippled from years of idle kicking. She squared her shoulders.

"We can start by moving all these to face the front!"

"Not the *desks*?" cried Mrs Ling. "But we *always* have them facing in two different directions in the big room—so you can take one half of the class, and your husband the other."

"Really? Well, *I'm* Headmistress now, and I do things *my* way!"

When they had finished, Mrs Higdon rang the bell and the children filed in dejectedly. Most of them didn't give the new master and mistress a second glance—Just another pair of teachers at the start of another term. How many more interminable terms before they could get out and start earning? Mrs Higdon knew the symptoms. She switched on an oxy-acetylene smile and went into battle. "Good morning, children!"

"Mornin', Missus Kingdom," they droned back. Harry Ellis the postman had faithfully delivered the wrong information all round the village.

"*Kingdom*?" said the Headmistress. "I think that's a little ambitious, don't you!" Tom's lips twitched. He pulled on his moustache and looked severe.

"HIGDON," said his wife, and chalked it up on the board in huge capitals. "You won't forget *that* in a hurry! Now, the registers!"

As she ticked off the names of seventy or so children ranging from four to fourteen, she looked keenly at each, committing the face to memory. "Marjory Ling?" She smiled enquiringly at the infants' teacher. "Your daughter, Mrs Ling?"

"Oh, no, Madam. My niece. *My* husband's the Sexton. Marjory's father is his brother—the bootmender." She made this sound a very inferior occupation. Mrs Higdon gave her a sideways look, then beamed at Marjory, a fresh-faced child with a thick frizz of biscuit-coloured hair held back by an Alice band.

"A bootmender? Splendid! Warm, dry feet are essential to the learning process. Cold feet, cold brain, that's what I always say!" She had already noticed that several pupils obviously couldn't afford to get their boots mended, and suspected that many of the absentees had no boots at all. She came to the last name. "Dora Watson! *Dora Watson!*"

"Yuzumm," mumbled a sulky voice. Mrs Higdon's head flicked up sharply. She took in a pale, empty face as sealed up and stupid as an egg, uncombed fair hair, the vacant eyes of an idiot child. But the eyes were rimmed with red. She made a note to investigate further.

Dora let out a sigh of relief as the teacher turned away. If I keep this up much longer, my face will drop off, she thought. I only hope it works.

"Now!" resumed Mrs Higdon. "I like to begin the day with a hymn!" She strode over to the battered piano and tried an experimental chord. It sounded like somebody rattling a bag full of broken glass. Undaunted, she plonked herself down on the stool with the air of a waggoner commanding a team of horses, and drew an almighty breath. "Let's give 'Onward Christian Soldiers' a shot, shall we? Off you go! One—Two—Three!"

Off they went, Mrs Higdon kneading the keys with short sturdy fingers and stamping on the loud pedal with both feet at once. During the second chorus, the door opened. Mrs Higdon did not register the gliding entrance of a slight, thin faced man dressed all in black, but her pupils did, and the singing started to waver. After a couple of bars, it petered out altogether.

"What on earth—?" The Headmistress rotated on her stool, face crinkling with vexation.

"May I present myself?" said the man in black in the voice of one accustomed to the bearing of bad news or coffins. "The Reverend Charles Tucker Eland. School Manager and Rector of Burston."

"Excellent!" cried the Headmistress, jumping to her feet and thrusting out her hand. He placed his pale palm limply on hers—it was like handling a halibut, she said afterwards, fresh off the slab. She wrung it warmly, half expecting it to squirm up into the air and flip into his pocket. "Just the man I want to see! I've drawn up a list of urgent repairs to the school . . ."

"All in good time, Mrs Higdon." The cold fingers disengaged themselves and the Rector swivelled his eyes over the ranks of children. His tongue flicked in and out, wetting thin lips. "I am here simply to wish you well in your studies."

His mouth bent itself into the shape of a smile, and the children nearest to him quailed. Taking this as his due, he paced forward, his eyes grinding round in their sockets. As he passed each one, legs trembled under petticoats and knees inside knickerbockers knocked.

He paused in front of tiny Emily Wilby. Her eyes stretched wide with terror as the black back stooped soundlessly and the pale face hovered an inch from her own. Then a black tentacle whipped out and a white finger hooked itself through a hole in her apron. "*Slattern!*" hissed the Reverend, and tugged hard, turning the tear into a great jagged rip. "Tsk! Tsk!" he exclaimed, unfolding himself into a black column of disapproval. "Someone had better be busy with her needle tonight!"

He turned back to Mrs Higdon. "Carry on! We shall meet again in church, no doubt?"

"I shall look in, certainly," replied the Headmistress evenly, "but Mr Higdon and I prefer to attend Chapel." The Rector's jaw dropped open with a click as if someone had pulled a pin out of the hinge. What little colour there was in his cheeks shrivelled out of them. He looked like a corpse waiting to have its jaw bound up. A corpse with cold, angry eyes. It spoke.

"The place of a schoolmistress on a Sunday is at church."

Mrs Higdon smiled. "If I may tolerate your beliefs, Rector, I am sure you can find space for mine. That is the Christian way. I hate a bigot, worse than a snake. Don't you agree?"

The Rector's jaw dropped even wider, then clicked shut. His tiny eyes glinted, the tips of two icicles. He twitched — a nod of dismissal — and turned to make his exit.

"Violet Potter!" bawled Mrs Higdon in a voice that would have set a regiment jogging. A small, solid girl sprang to attention, pushing back floppy dark hair behind her ears.

"Door, please — for the Reverend Charles Tucker Eland."

Violet scuttled to obey. The Rector faltered fractionally, then resumed his jointless progress from the room.

"One moment, Reverend!"

Eland froze in mid-stride, like a drawing on an Egyptian wall. "Yes?" he enquired through clenched teeth, determined not to turn round.

"The boot club," said the Headmistress. Eland wobbled. "For the children to save up for new footwear," she went on. "You do *have* one, I take it?" Unable to control the wobble, Eland turned it into a purposeful lunge and swerved round to face her.

"We have. It is open *only* to those who regularly attend church."

"I see. Only regular churchgoers possess feet? Miraculous!"

Eland's face clouded like a pan of boiling milk.

"Those are the terms of membership. Of course, more children would be likely to attend worship if their *Headmistress* were there to set an example."

His point scored, and before she could ruin his exit a third time, he rotated swiftly and slid out into the yard.

There was a sudden and bowel-dissolving scream.

"It's Mabel, Miss!" cried Violet, then put her apron over her face and whispered: "She's in — the *privy*!"

Everybody heard the whisper. There was a stampede for

the door. Mrs Higdon threw herself in its path and bellowed "*Back*!" They backed. A rogue elephant would have thought twice before charging Mrs Higdon. When she chose, she had a voice capable of starting and stopping avalanches.

"Take over, Mr Higdon!" she ordered, and swept outside. As she did so, a small, terrified figure, red ringlets askew and petticoats flapping, bolted out of a stinking hut at the end of the yard, skidded through the slush and hurtled to conceal itself in the folds of Mrs Higdon's voluminous skirt. Eland stood transfixed, rigid with outraged modesty.

"Don't let them get me! Don't let them get me!" came a muffled squeal from within the black serge.

"Let who get you?" asked the mistress, anxiously studying the pale agonized face in which all the freckles had been frightened from ginger to pale pink. "Is somebody *in* there?"

"Swingy things!" gibbered Mabel. "Dead and swingy things!"

"You wicked girl!" Eland was trembling all over, as if he, rather than Mabel had just escaped from a smelly box full of unnameable horrors. "What d'you mean by giving us such a fright?"

Mrs Higdon's eyes fired torpedos of anger and he retreated hastily. She turned back to Mabel. "There, there, dear," she murmured. "It's all right now. Can you tell us what happened?"

Mabel gulped. "I were just sitting down . . ." The Rector cleared his throat and studied a magpie on a distant rooftop. "I were just sitting down . . . when they come at me out of the dark!"

"What came at you?" asked Tom, emerging from the classroom.

"The dead things," whimpered Mabel. "The swinging things. They hit me in the face . . ."

"Mr Higdon, go and look," ordered the Head. Screwing up his face at the prospect, Tom stooped and entered the privy. They heard a stifled exclamation, then roars of laughter.

"They're dead all right!" boomed his voice. And he came out, holding up by the feet two swinging corpses.

It was a brace of fat and rotting pheasants.

"Well, they didn't walk there!" chuckled Tom as he and his wife sipped their cocoa during break. "George Durbidge must have had them in that gunny sack of his — poached, of course. Up comes the local bobby and he stows them in the first likely place!"

"He should know better, with his own daughter in school."

"A strange man. A self-made man," mused Tom. "Doesn't give a fig for anyone's opinion. Could be a bad enemy."

"Or a staunch friend, if it suited him. Well, time will tell. Meanwhile, those poor birds deserve a decent burial! And if he wants them back, he can answer to me!"

After break, Mrs Ling led Baby and the other infants into the smaller of the two rooms which made up the school, and Mrs Higdon took charge in the other. Tom banked up the fire and opened all the windows, then stationed himself at the back to keep an eye on the older boys, while the Headmistress set the whole group an essay: "What I want to do with my life."

The compositions were of varying quality, bearing in mind the age range, but one stood out. When she dismissed the children for dinner, Mrs Higdon summoned Dora Watson.

"Would you care to explain this?" she enquired, waving the blank sheet of paper. Dora was ready for her.

"Couldn't wroite nuthin'," she said, her face equally blank.

"Why not? Don't you know what you want to do with your life?"

"Don't care," said Dora, intensifying the imbecile stare.

"You don't care?" said the Headmistress. "That's a pity. Because I do. So let's sit down, and try again."

"We'll be sat yere all day then. Oi can't wroite."

The Headmistress's eyes gleamed. "Are you being cheeky?"

"Don't mean to be, Miss."

"Madam!" snapped the teacher. "You will call me Madam, or Governess, and my husband Mr Higdon. Is that clear?"

"Yes, Governess. But it won't make no diff'rence. Look in yer register. Ain't had hardly no schoolin' since we come here."

"*AHA*! I knew it! So you can turn off the fake accent this minute, and don't you *ever* insult your classmates again with that country bumpkin impersonation! Now, start writing!"

Dora sighed. "What did the others put?" she asked.

"Sadly, most of the girls said that they would go into service until they married. They don't yet realize there are other options. Come along, get writing, I'm hungry."

Dora sat down. Resting her cheek on her arm, she cradled the paper protectively and wrote, very slowly and laboriously:

i amm goan two bee in serviss wen i groe upp i wont too leev skule ass quik ass posibbel

The Headmistress pulled her marking pencil out from her straggly grey bun and wrote something on the bottom.

"*Magnificent*?" said Dora, eyes rounding in amazement.

"Quite magnificent. Nothing wrong with your reading either!"

"Seen that word before," said Dora, realizing her mistake.

"I'm sure you have. But you don't think it a fair comment?"

"It can't be, there's not one word in there spelled — " She shut her lips hurriedly.

"Spelled correctly?" finished Mrs Higdon. "Exactly! It takes a very clever little girl to make so many deliberate errors all in one go. Now why would a clever girl pretend to be stupid?"

"I'm not pretending! I'm dumb — unteachable!"

"There may be teachers who can't teach, but there is no

such thing as an unteachable child. And I'll eat my umbrella if you're one! Stubborn, yes." She looked at her so hard, Dora was sure she must be able to see her bones growing. "Don't you *want* to learn? D'you want to shut out the world and live like a beast in a pen who never knows there is anything beyond its feeding trough? You know what happens to animals like that?"

"They get eaten. But nobody's going to eat *me*!"

"Don't be so sure. It's a hungry, greedy world out there, only too eager to gobble up the ignorant. You need all the words and all the wits I can give you." Dora pursed her lips. Mrs Higdon tried another tack. "The law requires you attend school until you are fourteen or your parents will go to jail. Of course, certain special children . . ." She paused, as if considering a very bizarre notion. "But that hardly applies to *you* . . ."

"*What* doesn't apply?" asked Dora.

"Certain *special* children can take an examination if they need to leave school early . . . But it's a very hard exam. On the strength of this effort . . ." She looked disparagingly at Dora's essay and shook her head. Dora plucked at her sleeve.

"You mean, if I pass this exam, I can leave ho — school?"

"*If* you pass it? You haven't a hope, my dear."

"Yes I have! I bet I could do it! Let me write the composition again — now! I'll stay in all dinner-time!"

"As you wish . . ."

"And if it's good enough — "

"If it shows promise, then we shall have to work very hard together for the next months."

"And then you'll let me leave school?"

"When and if you pass the exam, yes." But by then, the Headmistress promised silently, you won't *want* to leave.

Dora laboured all through the dinner hour. She had abandoned her first idea — persuading Governess to let her stay at home and make herself indispensible to Dad so he wouldn't marry Ivy. Her only thought now was to get away altogether at the first opportunity. That would teach him. That was The Plan.

Mrs Higdon set off for the schoolhouse. The melting snow had softened the ground outside and Violet and one of the boys were having great fun turning it over with a couple of huge spades loaned (on disapproval) by the Sexton. As Annie bustled up the path she heard a bellow of anger.

"Callous little brute! Look at this, Governess!"

Tom shook his fist at the crestfallen boy who was gazing shamefaced at something by his feet. "Sliced a worm clean in half! And laughed when he saw it!"

Mrs Higdon put her hand on the boy's shoulder. She could feel every bump in it through the worn jacket. His pasty calves, sockless between the tops of his boots and the bottoms of sawn off trousers, were as thin as pea sticks. He was shivering with cold and disappointment.

"All life is sacred, Billy," she said. "You'll remember that another time, won't you?"

He nodded, snuffling.

"Good boy! Now, what we all need is something to eat!" She trotted into the house waving a brown paper parcel. The children followed. "What is it?" asked Violet.

"Bloaters! I nabbed a fish vendor on my way. You'll find the cutlery in my bag. Billy—you can be the chef! Stop gawping, Violet! If a girl can dig the garden, Billy can cook the dinner!"

Violet laid out the curious flat knives on the table and blew the dust off some plates from the cupboard. When the food was ready, Mrs Higdon served it out—taking only bread and cheese for herself—said Grace, and waited for them to begin.

"Well, tuck in! What's the matter?"

The tips of four ears went pink. Tom guessed the problem.

"Ticklish things, fish knives! But all the best people use them."

"We ain't the best people, though," said Billy.

"Well, you're going to be!" declared Mrs Higdon. "Everyone I teach is going to come out of school the best person he can be or I'll know the reason why! Tom—Demonstrate!"

"It was easy!" boasted Violet when she was back home. "I'll never let Mrs Fisher make me feel stupid again at Harvest Tea because I don't do things right. Like Governess said: If you don't know—Ask! Nobody can laugh at you for wanting to know."

"What else you done in school then?" enquired her mother, who had been out in the fields all day, wrenching up ice-baked swedes, and was eager for a bit of entertainment.

Violet pushed that wretched floppy hank of hair back behind her ear and plunged in:

"Mr Higdon's a bit fierce but really handsome, and he smokes this Tortoiseshell tobacco, and at break time he stood in the yard and we got in a circle, and he threw the tin up in the air and shouted: 'Scramble!' and we scrambled like mad and Emily got it, and she's going to use it for her dressmaking pins..."

"Dressmaking?" asked her mother warily.

"It's all right. Governess is giving us the material. And she's got a Singer sewing machine, the latest kind with pedals for your feet! Me and Marjory are making shirts and the little 'uns are doing red hankies, and anything we don't want we can sell to buy things for the school! Oh and she gave me *this*—"

Mrs Potter wiped her hands clean on her apron of darned sacking, opened the faded green book and turned the first page with a reverential and blistered finger.

"Is it foreign?" she asked, staring at the weird symbols.

"Pitman's Shorthand!" said Violet grandly. "For clerks and sec-etries! I'm going to go to her house at nights to learn it. It's all right, we don't have to pay—I can do washing-up and things, Governess *hates* housework, says she's always too busy. Anyway, after dinner, the donkey cart came from the station with all their personals in it, and you should see what they got! There's a big typewriter, took two of us to carry it in—and a violin and an American organ, and Marjory's going to learn to play it and if I bring Dad's concertina, we can have a school band!"

She broke off, temporarily dazzled, then rushed on: "And

her *books*, Mum! French, and Russian and all sorts, a real library! And in the afternoon while we sewed — the boys did figures with Mr Higdon — we made up stories, a line each, and then she got a camera out on a big tripod thing, and went behind it and stuck her head under this cloth, and there was a flash and it didn't half go bang! It's February the first, nineteen eleven, she said, and this is my first picture of you. We'll keep a record of how we all change as the years go by, and Mr Higdon will set up a dark room so you can print the photos yourselves!"

She stopped, out of steam. Her parents looked at each other over the dark head and smiled. Maybe, at long last, things were going to start looking up at Burston Council School.

CHAPTER 5

Dad came in late, very subdued. He gave Dora a quick glance — she was hunched over the kitchen table, scribbling excitedly, filling up sheets of paper — and went over to the stone sink in the scullery to wash his hands. When he came back, she had moved aside her story, (for the dinner-time composition had just grown and grown) and was ladling him out a bowl of soup. Not tomato, thank God, he thought, shuddering.

"Good day?" he asked.

She shrugged. "All right, I suppose."

He nodded, relieved, and put his head down, spooning the soup in hungrily, gasping as it burned his mouth. He's not going to ask anything else, Dora thought furiously. Well, see if I care. I don't want him to know about The Plan anyway. But she would have liked to have read him just a bit of the story, because Mrs Higdon had been really pleased with it.

Dad was frankly too tired to talk. He'd arrived at Ford's place well before dawn and waited outside, cap in hand, listening to the bang and clatter of crockery as the farmer forked down bacon and eggs and swilled mug after mug of tea. Out he came at last — swearing fruitily and with considerable invention. Hoisting an oil lamp, he led the way through the snow slushed mud to the cowsheds.

As the door creaked open, the smell smacked Fred in the face. It was like putting his head into a bucket of ripe Camembert. He couldn't see the cows at first, but he heard them, shuddering and moaning and munching in the dark. Slobbering at one end and plopping at the other. The straw underfoot was as slimy as if it had been chewed — or worse. Ford lifted the lamp, and its pale light streaked the flanks of big, saggy beasts and yellowed the whites of baleful eyes. He set it down and handed Fred a bucket.

"Start on Dahlia," he said, shoving him on to the stool. "She's a real gusher, you'll soon get the knack."

Fred stared at the bulging udder. The teats on it were as big as his fingers. Gritting his teeth, he put out a hand and gave one a tentative tug. Nothing. He yanked harder.

"What d'you think you're doing?" Ford came stamping over. "Ringing the church bells? You'll get nothing out of her that way except a kick round the ear. Like this, boy." And, resting his face against Dahlia's smelly flank, he closed his eyes and reached upward. Milk tinged into the bucket. Dahlia gushed.

"Didn't know I was a dairy maid, did you?" guffawed the farmer. "Now clean up all this mucky straw, then come over and join the threshers."

Ford was very proud of his steam threshing machine — the only one in the district. When Fred arrived, the machine was already in action, chomping and belching and blowing out clouds of dust. Fred joined Mr Potter on top of the oat stack — a bristling fortress erected the previous autumn — and they hurled down more sheaves to be fed into the mechanical belly. Straw poured out of her rear end and was rapidly built into another stack as the first one dwindled under their feet.

When they were almost on ground level, they heard a sound like a million whistling kettles all going off at once, and the floor beneath them heaved, releasing a torrent of rats and mice who had been wintering inside the stack. Fred jumped out of the way with a yelp. He knew now why Potter had tied his trousers below the knees with string. Ten minutes' break was allowed for a drink of cold tea, then they moved on round all the farms, until dusk.

Ford was well pleased with the day's work. "You're in for a treat now, boy," he said as they trudged back into the yard. And the fat farmer led the way to the killing shed.

The men stood around in the gloom, sleeves rolled up, silent and watchful. To Fred's surprise, the stranger from the Crown Inn was there too.

Henry Garnham, Ford's brother-in-law, stepped forward, a spare, wiry figure in a dark, three piece suit. Carefully removing his jacket, he handed it to his son Herbert, who folded it over his arm. Then he took off his tall felt billycock hat, revealing sparse brown hair in curious contrast to a white, sharp-cornered beard, and handed that over too, turning his cuffs back above thin, veined arms. He put out his hand with a surgeon's gesture and Herbert placed the handle of a huge sledgehammer into it. Now Ford took up a smaller mallet called a felling hammer, and tested it against his palm. They might have been preparing for a game of croquet on the Rectory lawn.

Bessie was led in on a tether, twenty-six gleaming stones of her, the colour of Greek marble. Ford patted her flank fondly: he had watched her grow from a piglet no bigger than a baby's fist, with a tiny wrinkled snout like a furled rosebud. Bessie rubbed against his leggings, grunting affectionately. Then she saw the knife and whetstone hanging at his belt — and she began to squeal.

The squealing of a pig is a terrible sound, high and hysterical, like a machine out of control. Her eyes rolled and she hauled on the tether. The man on the other end hauled back, his heels skidding through the sawdust.

"You bloody fool!" Ford threw his own twenty-seven stones at Bessie, and sat down hard on her, grabbing the rope and twisting it round her snout. The squeals cut off abruptly. Bessie stopped struggling, just stood there, legs braced, her eyes vanishing backwards into their sockets. Ford flung the free end of the rope at Fred, bawling, "Tie that off!" Then, with the agility of a ballerina he jumped up, lifted his mallet and placed it against her forehead. As he indicated the spot, Garnham's sledgehammer swung up — and round — and down.

Fred turned away. There was a dull thock of bone and flesh and the sound of something heavy toppling sideways. "Get the back legs!" yelled Ford, and in an instant she was hanging, stunned, snout downwards from a hook in the rafter.

"Make ready with the buckets!"

Out of the tail of his eye, Fred saw a knifegleam scythe the air. He heard the guzzle of throatflesh as it found its mark, and Ford grunting and swearing as he levered down on the hilt. There was a long sigh of anticipation, then whoops of applause. He stumbled outside, heaving.

"Are you all right, Fred?" It was Tom Higdon.

Fred hauled a gulp of cold air into his lungs. "Just about."

"Your first slaughtering? Know how you feel. Never cared much for them myself." He waited for the man to recover. "Listen, I didn't introduce myself properly. I'm the new schoolmaster . . ."

"The new . . .?"

"If you're interested. I'm calling a few men together to —"

"*There* you are!" It was Ford, glowing with pride, mutton chop whiskers spangled with red droplets, arms slobbered with wetness, leggings dappled as if he had been dancing in a vat of wine. "Curdles your belly, does it?" he chortled, streaky bacon jowls jumping with amusement. "Killing's a part of farm life, boy. Birthing and deathing, that's our stock in trade."

He slapped Fred on the back hard enough to rearrange several vital organs, then gripped his hand between fat red trotters. "You'll soon toughen up. I'll see you tomorrow?"

"Yes," muttered Fred thickly, pulling his hand back as soon as he dared, and averting his eyes from the bulky shape swinging in the lamplight behind the farmer.

"Right!" Ford's eyes rolled round to the other man. "And as for you — get back to your schoolbooks. You've no business here."

Fred almost ran from the yard. When he came to the pump, he pulled off his jacket and scrubbed away Ford's pawprint under the stinging water. I'll toughen up, he promised, I'll learn how to kill. But I'll never like it . . .

Spring sent green shivers through the countryside, and the pear tree at the back of the school exploded into a huge white sneeze. Even the Reverend Eland seemed to be afflicted with spring fever. Whenever he "looked in" to see how lessons were going, he developed a sort of nettle rash and could hardly keep still for irritation.

"I think it most unseemly, Governess," he reproved on one occasion, "for the teachings of the Bible to be made into a children's *game*."

"Christ was a story-teller," came the reply. "And wasn't it his wish that we should all become as little children?"

"There's a difference between child*like* and child*ish*, Mrs Higdon. And how, pray, do you justify inviting a travelling player into class at a time scheduled for mental arithmetic?"

"Ah, yes! Violet, tell Mr Eland how many performances the Punch and Judy man gives in a year if he does three a week?"

"A hundred and fifty-six, Madam!"

"Correct! Marjory, how many pairs of shoes will he wear out, if — "

"Never mind!" interrupted the Rector. "Point taken! *Good morning*, Madam!"

"A most ungracious woman," agreed Mrs Eland when he arrived home smoking with irritation. "I dropped by last week to see how needlework was progressing, and she didn't stand up when I came in!"

One Monday in June, Mrs Higdon set everyone an essay on what they had done over the weekend. Dora sucked on her pencil for five minutes and wrote:

"It was baking hot. Dad should have been in the fields with the other men, but he got married instead. So he's lost a day's pay, and Ivy is now Mrs Fred Watson. Her dress was very elegant, a sort of long white tube with a veil and a coronet of lilies. Dad looked clumsy standing next to her. He plastered his hair back with water, but it kept jumping up in sprigs. And the sleeves of his jacket were too short. Baby was bridesmaid. Mrs Eland called her a real little cherub all but the wings. Ivy likes Mrs Eland because

Rector earns four hundred and ninety-five pounds a year plus the rents off fifty-four acres of Glebe land. (She looked him up in *Crockford's Directory*) and lives in a house with twenty rooms. Baby ate too much afterwards and was sick."

Dora bit her pencil and thought about what happened next . . . Ivy had taken off the lovely gown and put it away in mothballs at the back of the wardrobe. Then, in her old dress and a spotless apron crunching with starch, she got down on her hands and knees and scrubbed the cottage from top to bottom. Dora pitched in, dragging buckets of dusty water out through the back to be emptied into a hole under the hedge. She didn't mind hard work, but there seemed something terribly heartless about it. Ivy was acting like some kind of Florence Nightingale, disinfecting the premises of all traces of the previous wife.

Dora's pencil started to skitter across the page.

"Dad's taken down all Mum's pictures, so as not to upset Ivy, but I kept one. She's at a picnic. Her hair's all over the place and her mouth is open and laughing. Dad's gone on the land and Ivy doesn't approve because Mrs Eland looks down on labourers, so she says it's only for now and to do with his artistic temperament. She says he's getting coarse, and just because he works in the fields, he doesn't have to act like a peasant . . ."

She stopped, considering this. Dad had definitely changed since he'd started labouring. He was always tired, for one thing. Maybe it was the contrast with Ivy who was so fussy and efficient that made him seem suddenly vulgar and oafish. Like one of the neighbours said, "That woman would starch the sunlight if it stayed still long enough!"

But the harder Ivy tried to change him, the more obstinate he became. It was as if he were punishing himself for his wife's death. He'd made a vow and he was going to stick to it, and if people said it was making him common, then by golly, he'd *be* common.

Dora sort of understood this, because she was obstinate too, but the awful fact was, he was getting to be embarrassing. Her big, ugly, lovable old Dad could sometimes be so stupid it made her want to weep with humiliation. She lifted her pencil and tried to make sense of it.

"When we have tea at the Rectory, he goes all clumsy and spills things and eats with his mouth open. I think he does it to annoy Mr Eland, but if it's a joke, why doesn't he *tell* me? I don't think it can be, because the first time he did it, I laughed and he looked upset. Anyway, he's started doing it at home. Or maybe he always did. I know he does it more when he catches me watching . . ."

She saw Governess coming and hastily flipped over the page, scribbling on the back: "I'm eleven now. Can I take my exam?"

"Maybe next year," said Mrs Higdon. "You know, you have quite a gift with words. You should keep a diary, and write down all the interesting things which happen to you here and at home."

So you can spy on me, thought Dora. I'll just write about school then. You don't have to worry about taking sides when you're in school.

Or so she thought.

CHAPTER 6

The year whirled round and the diary filled up amazingly. Harvest, Bonfire Night, Christmas, New Year, something was always happening, but Dora's favourite items were those involving Mrs Higdon. One in particular made her laugh over and over:

February 1912. The Harriers came and asked if the boys could have a half day to join them because it's the custom. Mrs H made a noise like a buffalo with a gag on. "We must all bow to custom, must we not?" she said. "Very well. But if any boy cares for better work than hunting an innocent hare to death, he is welcome to stay here with the girls."

Just then, E. slithered in. "Tradition, Mrs Higdon, is the life blood of a village community," he said. And she replied, "Tell that to the hare when it's splattering the countryside with ITS life blood!" Seventeen boys opted to stay behind.

That second summer, the Rector held a garden party. While it was in progress, other things were happening of which Dora was unaware, but which would have made excellent reading...

"Welcome to our humble home, Governess! *Such* an honour!"

Mrs Eland, splendid in oyster satin, surged over the Rectory lawn, brandishing her croquet mallet. Annie Higdon frowned. Surely the Rector's wife couldn't be balancing a *tea tray* on her head, laden with cream cakes? Ah no — just another new hat.

"Perhaps we might also entice you into church one day?" simpered her hostess. Mrs Higdon smiled.

"You forget, Mrs Eland, *my* husband is also a preacher."

"A *lay* preacher," corrected Eland, sidling up.

"Nobody minds him preaching in *chapel*," rumbled Ford as he lumbered over with a plate of sausage rolls. "So long as he leaves off preaching at my men when they're trying to work."

"Not to mention . . ." Fisher was close behind, licking his fingers. ". . . preaching Socialism to his *pupils!*"

"I beg your pardon?" Eland blinked rapidly. "Politics — in the *classroom?*"

Fisher nodded. "Innocent children. It's taking an unfair advantage of his position." His teeth closed round a crustless cucumber sandwich, and his dental plate squeaked.

"And aren't *you* taking an unfair advantage?" demanded Mrs Higdon. "Slandering my husband behind his back?"

"Where *is* the good Mr Higdon?" queried the Rector.

"At a meeting — with friends."

"And we all know what kind of meeting!" gloated Fisher.

"Ah! Here's Mrs Watson!" trilled the Rector's wife in tones of relief. "And the dear little girls! Such dear little dresses with blue sashes! But is dear *Mr* Watson not with you?"

Ivy's face went as pink and closed-in as a sugared almond.

"He's at a meeting — with friends," she replied tersely. She knew full well what Fred was up to and she didn't like it one bit. Mrs Eland was her only friend. She didn't want to lose her.

"Political discussions outside school are one thing," said Eland, tactfully glossing over her embarrassment. "But *inside* — Growing minds are so receptive to the wrong ideas."

"Let's get this clear!" rapped Mrs Higdon. "In *my* school, I preach the Gospel. And if Christ's ideas are so terrifyingly close to Socialism, perhaps you'd do well to rethink your own!"

Mrs Eland gave a shrill giggle. "You have such a strong, independent mind, Mrs Higdon! Almost masculine!" She preened and adjusted her hat. "*Do* tell us your educational theories. What can you offer our young people for the future? In three words!"

"Three words? Very well — Bread and roses."

"Roses?" Mrs Eland fluttered her lashes in genteel bewilderment. "D'you mean like the ones on my hat?"

Mrs Higdon looked at it.

"No," she said. "Superficially perhaps. But yours have no scent. Because they aren't real. Excuse me!" And she strode off.

"Well!" pouted Mrs Eland. "Did *you* understand that, Dora?"

Dora blushed. "I think she meant — flowers of the spirit."

"Did she indeed?" muttered Eland. "And what does she think *I'm* here for?" He bit into a celery stalk and crunched it slowly with a sound like necks being twisted.

Fisher flapped his napkin warningly. "She told them about the French Revolution — and we all know what that led to."

"I must say," fluted Mrs Eland, "it's bad enough our young folk learning about these dreadful rebels and tub thumpers. I never thought I'd see the day they were being *taught* by them!" She whirred her lashes at Ford.

The farmer shoved in a sausage roll and voiced his conclusion through a mouthful of crumbs. "Higdon's the troublemaker. She's only a teacher, after all. And a woman at that!" And he rambled off to restock his plate.

Dora took the opportunity to catch up with Mrs Higdon.

"Governess — Madam — Can I ask you a question?"

"You may, Dora, and the answer is no, not yet."

"But I'm twelve now, and I already read better than Violet."

"Patience, dear. Come and sniff this glorious honey-suckle."

"No, thank you, Madam." Dora wandered away. And found herself asking why it was that she felt suddenly *relieved* . . .

"To sum up," said Tom Higdon, "the union will campaign for higher wages, laying-off payments in bad weather, and for the farmers to provide tools. Are we agreed?" The answering roar left him in no doubt.

Clutching her father's hand, Violet gazed up at the teacher in awe. Gone were his classroom mannerisms — the nervous tugging on the braces and moustache — now, standing on a crate in the middle of the Long Meadow, he seemed almost luminous with power.

"Are we not MEN?" he shouted. "And equal all in the sight of God? We ask for nothing but what is ours by right! Reward for our labours, and recognition of our worth! We demand only what has been stolen from us over the centuries — our pride, our manhood and our freedom! Bread and roses, lads, bread and roses!"

And a shout went up to scatter the stars:

"BREAD AND ROSES!"

"I'm glad you came, Violet," called Higdon as they cycled back together, headlamps jousting through the dark. "I always knew you were a fighter! How d'you feel about doing a bit of teaching yourself next term? Just the little ones to start?"

In answer, she rang her bell as loud as she could, and Potter rang his and Higdon joined in till the air tingled. As they whizzed round the corner, Tom put his heel down and stopped.

"Shhhhh! Listen!"

Two nightingales were calling to each other through the scented darkness. Tom listened, his face shining with wonder. Violet knew now that he was a most extraordinary and special man.

Ivy had no such illusions about Fred Watson, and told him as much on his return to Blossom Cottage.

"Union meetings! I didn't know where to put myself! Promise me you won't join. *Promise* me, Fred."

"I promise," he said sadly. *Little does she know*, he thought to himself, *there's only Tom Higdon wants me in anyway. The others all think I'm a spy for Eland and the farmers.*

In no time at all, two years had passed since the Higdon's arrival, and Dora's diary had filled up five exercise books. During the spring of 1913, somebody else started to keep a record. And that somebody found the affairs of the school, and of Mr and Mrs Higdon in particular, very interesting indeed...

PART 2: TERM OF TRIAL

It is but a short time ago
We all remember well
Two meetings in the schoolroom
Held a verdict for to tell.

He went round all the village
A few tales he did hear
He put them all together
And a blower he got there.

Then fancy Johnnie Philpot
To show his face up there
For when a boy he went to jail
For riding an old mare.

Can you call him a gentleman
Who called his flock a liar
And may the Lord have mercy on him
To save him from Hell fire.

If ever we knew a parson
To Burston ever came
Better than the Higdons
Then I am overcome.

Lines from a song made up by the villagers of Burston

CHAPTER I

"Clear the decks, Tom!—Suppertime!"

A laden tin plate swooped towards Higdon's immaculately ordered desk, and he whipped his notes out of the way just in time to save them from being turned into a placemat. "Tuck in while it's warm!" ordered his wife, plonking down the plate and heading for her own cosy chair where another dish was resting on the arm. She settled back with a book in one hand and a fork in the other, absent-mindedly jabbing at the food when she remembered, and carrying it to her mouth without looking. Most of it ended up on her front.

Tom examined his supper and blenched. Green lumps again . . . Oh, for a bowl of beef stew! No chance of that when the only beef Annie approved of was the sort that was still walking around. The farm workers pulled his leg mercilessly about it—and always laid an extra place when they saw him coming.

Sighing, he prodded a bullety sprout and it fired itself off the plate. He let out something close to an oath.

"Food all right, dear?" murmured Annie, turning a page and stabbing the arm of her chair with her fork.

"Fine, dear. Lovely," muttered Tom from under the table.

There was a knock at the door. Annie got up, nose still in book, the fringe of her shawl trailing across her plate.

"Hello, Violet! Who's this you've brought with you?"

"We met on the doorstep, Ma'am." It was Noah Sandy, one of the local smallholders. "Not disturbin' you, am I?"

"Of course not! Come in out of this mad March wind!"

Noah wiped his boots carefully and pulled off his cap. Violet headed straight for the typewriter and started clacking away with a businesslike air.

"Tom, look who's—" Annie stared round in puzzlement.

There was a scuffling sound, a clunk and a groan as Higdon banged his head on the underside of the desk. He emerged backwards and red in the face, wiping furtive fingers.

"Dropped my — er — pen. Well, take a seat, man!"

Noah sat down, twisting his cap between chapped fingers.

"The fact is," he blurted out, "I'm sick to the back teeth of fighting the Parish Council." Noah was the only Council member who wasn't a farmer. "I've been trying to push them into fixing the footpaths and the old bridge — not to mention making some of them hovels of cottages fit to live in — but they vote me down every time. They don't give a — a *blow* about Burston."

Annie snorted agreement. "Just like the School Managers! The trouble I had getting them to install a new heating system, and even now the wretched thing doesn't work properly!"

"Well, I know you've spent your own money time and again," ventured Noah. The Headmistress twitched her shawl dismissively.

"If the children need things, what else can — " She stopped, her face wrinkling with bewilderment. "Gracious! My shawl's all wet! However did that . . .?"

"What can we do for you, Noah?" interrupted Tom.

"Well — " Noah cleared his throat. "You and Governess are liked here. Admired. And everybody knows how much better things have been since you got the unions going. Now, the elections are coming up, and if *you* stood for Council, Tom, I reckon you'd get in. Then maybe we could work together to get things done."

Tom reached for his pipe. "Two of us? Against the farmers? Not a hope! We'd need a whole new Council — made up of working men . . . " He tapped the stem of the pipe against his teeth. "We could do it, mind, if folks were prepared to stand behind us." His eyes gleamed. "We could take over the whole show!"

"Hold on," said Noah. "We don't want you getting into trouble. I know what happened to you in Wood Dalling . . . "

The typewriter stopped. "*I* don't," said Violet Potter.

Husband and wife exchanged glances. "Go on," said Annie. "Tell her!"

"They kicked us out, Violet," said Tom. "For doing just what I'm planning to do now."

Violet's eyes went as round as gobstoppers.

"But why? It's got nothing to do with school."

"That's what *they* said. They reckoned teachers had no business poking into local affairs, so they trumped up a lot of charges against us, and gave us the boot. Rough justice, eh?"

"That's not justice!" said Violet. "That's revenge!"

"What did I say?" laughed Tom. "She's a natural born rebel!"

"Who was Gamble?" pursued Violet, emboldened. Like everyone else, she'd heard rumours about the Higdons' previous troubles.

"Oh, that's another story!" Mrs Higdon sat down on Tom's desk and swung her legs, remembering. "He was a farmer, of course. Couldn't stand Tom, could he, dear? He was always poaching children out of his classes to work in the fields — and him a School Manager too! We warned him over and over, but it did no good. Then one afternoon, Tom looked up, and there was Gamble with little Alfred Cottrell leading his horse right past the window bold as brass, and grinning all over his ugly face. That did it! Tom jumped up—"

"I jumped up!" Tom interrupted. "I ran into the field, knocked the beggar down, and pushed him in the muck where he belonged!"

Mrs Higdon clapped her hands delightedly, her crumpled face flushed with girlish adoration. Then she remembered her dignity. "Of course he was taken to court and fined heavily. And rightly so. Violence doesn't solve anything."

Noah looked worried. "Perhaps it would be better if we forget all about this Parish Council business," he said.

"No backing down, Noah!" Tom was fired up now and crackling like a rick. "You know I'm the only man for the job. Don't worry — we'll do this strictly by the book. We'll capture that Council fair and square, with working men as candidates and working men to vote for 'em — if I have to drag them out of the fields myself! Blow it, man, it *is* 1913!"

Violet was fast asleep by the time they finished talking, so Tom wrapped her up in a blanket and carried her home. In her dreams she was riding high on his shoulders, drinking in shouts and whistles of applause. And because she was so high up, higher than everyone else, she saw them first. The dark shadows. Coiling and simmering in their path...

She shouted to warn him, but the cheering was so loud he couldn't hear. And she *knew*, she saw so clearly that the shadows were going to get him, and that she could do *nothing* to stop them. She felt him stumble and start to pitch forward, and then she was falling too, and no one to catch her, for the cheering faces had all dissolved into the shadows, and she was crashing, tumbling down into the darkness...

"*VIOLET*! Wake up! It's gone seven!"

She kicked back the blanket and sat up, mouth dry, heart kicking, a question rattling her brain like rain on tin.

"Why didn't anybody HELP?"

"Evening, Reverend! Good to see you! Take a seat!"

"No, thank you." Eland gave a little cough, and straightened his coat tails. "I believe I have a place *reserved*." And, lifting such chin as he possessed, he walked purposefully to the front of the hall to join the ranks of the incumbent Parish Councillors who, confident of re-election, were sitting all together, stout and sedate as a row of encyclopedias. Potter leaned forward and tapped Tom's shoulder.

"I see he thinks he's in already!"

A roomful of eyes shifted from Parson to Schoolmaster and back. It was election night, and everybody knew that they were *both* after a seat on the Parish Council.

For the first time in years the place was packed. Extra chairs had been set out for the new candidates and their supporters—men who, during the day, were hired servants to those dignitaries up at the front and paid their wages back to them in rent for slum cottages. But by the time everyone had arrived, it was standing room only.

Tom's tactics had worked—"I'll fight for you," he'd promised all those who had given up bothering to vote because the Council never did them any good, "but only if you fight for yourselves." Now, shoulder to shoulder they stood, in grimed, open-necked shirts, squaring up to the seated farmers in their collars of stiff celluloid. Uneasy but excited, they felt for the first time ever that they had a right to be in this room where decisions concerning all of them were made. It was a good feeling.

While the votes were taken and counted, Eland sat rigidly upright, knees nipped tightly together. Tom leaned forward, tugging at his moustache. At last came the longed for shout.

"Silence, please! The results of the election of new Parish Councillors are as follows . . . Tom Higdon tops the poll with thirty-one votes!"

There was an eruption of joy. Chairs went flying as the labourers pushed forward to slap their champion on the back.

"ORDER ! The remaining successful candidates are . . . " As each name was read out, the Rector's knees pinched more tightly, till he could have cracked open a walnut between them. The skin round his lips shirred with suppressed indignation. Every other winner except one farmer—good old Bob Ford—was a labouring man. Then Eland heard the name he had been waiting for, and his face went as pale as a peeled whelk.

"The Reverend Charles Tucker Eland—nine votes!" The face shrivelled inwards in an agony of rage and humiliation—someone had squirted neat vinegar on the whelk. Noah leapt up.

"I move that Tom Higdon be made Chairman! Come on, Tom!"

Higdon strode to the front.

"You've done me proud," he told his supporters. "And I

mean to do the same by you. From now on, part of your rents will go towards repairing your cottages, and together we'll work for a better Burston, a Burston that belongs to the *people*, with a school for your children they'll be happy and proud to attend!"

The members of the old Council were too shellshocked to speak, but Eland was knit up of tougher fibres. As the men, irrepressible now, surged round Tom, he squirmed to his feet, insinuating a moist, chilly hand into Tom's hot one.

"My felicitations," he breathed. "A notable victory. Might I point out, however — " he stifled a cry as his hat was knocked from his head by a brawny fist reaching across him to give Tom an affectionate punch " — that you have *not* been elected on to the board of School Managers, and that we *must* be consulted before making any alterations to the buildings or curriculum."

Eland's lips curved in an upside-down snarl. Tom grinned back. Their eyes met as each man recognized and acknowledged his enemy.

"Charles, dear, whatever do you make of this?"

The Reverend Eland paused in his deliberations. It was breakfast time in the Rectory, and he was faced with the first of many weighty decisions that would make up his day. Should he apply strawberry conserve (a gift from a grateful parishioner) or ginger marmalade to his freshly toasted muffin?

"What do I make of what, Light of my Existence?" he enquired, his knife hovering. She shook her newspaper at him.

"They're calling it the Burston Revolution! That business over the Council elections! Listen to this — *Parson's nose put out of joint!* D'you think that's meant to be funny?"

The knife clattered on to a rose patterned plate. Eland snatched the newspaper and thrust his face into it.

"Confound them!" he snarled. "They've made me look an utter fool!"

"I didn't realize you only got nine votes," said his wife

mildly, rescuing the knife and helping herself to a second muffin which she ate with restrained relish. "I thought you said Higdon beat you by a whisker."

"The number of votes is immaterial," snapped her husband. "It's the principle of the thing. Working men simply don't know what's good for them. How can I be a good shepherd if the flock start telling themselves what to do?"

"Gadarene swine," remarked his wife unexpectedly. He shot her a suspicious look. "Rushing headlong," she elaborated. "To their own destruction. You might put that in a sermon."

"If I need inspiration," he said tartly, "I shall seek it from a higher source than my own breakfast table, thank you very much."

He lifted and rang a small silver bell. The maid entered and began clearing away. Mrs Eland plucked ineffectually at the muffins as they were levitated out of reach. Eland glowered.

"I shall call a meeting of the School Managers," he informed her. "It's time *we* elected a new Chairman." The tiniest hint of a smile lifted the corners of his thin lips. "And once *I'm* elected, I rather think I might appoint you a Manageress too."

He caught hold of the maid's arm and indicated that she should return the muffins to the table. "How would you take to that idea?"

CHAPTER 2

On a tangy day at the start of another autumn, Mrs Higdon took the infants outside for open air dancing — "Beneficial to the body and stimulating to the brain!" as she had been informed by a visiting Inspector, who incidentally had written a splendid report of the school. She brought in her wind-up gramophone with its gigantic Morning Glory horn sprouting from a handsome mahogany case, and set it down in the middle of the playground.

Mabel Plumtree, whose mother would not allow her to take exercise on account of her having fallen down once and never been the same again, (though nobody could remember what she was like before) sat on a cushion, guarding the box of needles and making sure that each of the heavy black records, as big and brittle as old dinner plates, went back into its paper cover after use.

"Improvise!" boomed Mrs Higdon, turning up the volume of *Weel May The Keel Row*. "And keep moving! Too cold to dawdle!"

Inside, Tom was dancing too. Smelly Wittle would make anyone jump up and down. Smelly, or Jimmy as he had been christened, was ten years old and had been kept down with the infants until Mrs Ling flatly refused to have him a second longer. "Untouchable and unteachable" she called him.

So Smelly was sulking. He always sulked. It was what the scraggy, flea-bitten child did second best. Everybody knew what he did *best*. Nobody would sit within a yard of him. He knew why, of course. He knew, and he minded. Minded so badly that he had made his smell into a sort of armour, protective at first and then defiant. It was all he had. He only came to school to keep out of his dad's way.

While Tom struggled to get him to count up to four on his fingers, Jimmy sat there, willing himself it seemed to stink more strongly, until Higdon withdrew in disgust and turned his attention to Sam Todd.

But if Jimmy was bad, Sam was unbearable. He was twelve years old, well fleshed and confident, and he could barely read his name. Not that he cared, because he was going to take over his father's farm one day.

Tom tried to interest him in a storybook with animals in it, but as soon as he found a word he knew, Sam went off into his own world, filling the room with cattle and horses, cracking an imaginary whip and shouting, "Whoa, Blossom! Keep your tail up, Diamond!" to everyone's vast amusement. When Tom turned his back to write on the board, Sam grabbed some red chalk, smeared it all over his hands, and waggled them at the horrified master, yelling, "I killed fifteen pigs this mornin'!"

"You'll kill no more today!" raged Tom. "Look at this book! Ruined! All over fingerprints! You can stay in after school!"

"Can't stop!" was the staggering reply. "Got to get back to the men. They'll be idling if I'm not there to shout at 'em."

"I can see I shall have to go and shout at your father!"

"Like to see you try! He's a big man. Higher than three haystacks, and he's got a bigger voice than you. A great big voice like you need for crow scaring. I go crow scaring too—"

"Well, let's hear your great big voice now. Wipe your fingers clean and read to me from the top of page two."

"But I ain't killed all the pigs yet. Got one more to do."

The pink flesh of the boy's neck creaked as he looked round menacingly, and everyone shrank back. "Jest a little one . . ." And, flexing his fingers, he sprang on to a terrified and suddenly wide awake Jimmy Wittle and sank them into the wizened throat, bawling, "That's the way! Catch the blood in a bucket!" Jimmy's skinny legs flailed desperately from the bottoms of his cut-down trousers, and he gargled with terror.

"Stop that! STOP THAT AT ONCE!" roared Tom, vaulting over his desk and hauling the boys apart. He snatched up his cane and swung it high over their cringing shoulders.

"TOM!"

Higdon froze, his arm up, like a conductor shot in the back half-way through a concerto. Mrs Higdon was standing in the doorway, her face as white as her husband's was purple.

"Don't do that, Tom," she said, her voice terribly quiet. Then she walked over and, reaching up on tiptoe, removed the stick from between his fingers and placed it on his desk. The whole class heard it rattle as she set it down, so intense and chilling a silence had fallen upon the room. The six-foot master suddenly looked like a schoolboy caught out lobbing tin tacks on an elastic band.

He turned his back on the class and muttered, "Drat it, Annie, d'you have to correct me in front of them?"

"I won't have you thrashing them, Tom."

"But they've got to learn!"

"Learn what? That angry grown-ups lay into them when it's not their fault? Jimmy's learned that already—at home!"

"I'll tell my dad on you!" yelled Sam, seizing his chance.

"Send him to me," returned Tom. "I'll thrash him as well!"

"*Mr Higdon!*" The little woman drew herself up to her full height—just level with Tom's shoulder. "May I remind you *who* is Head of this school?"

Tom looked as if he were about to burst. "And I'm never to be allowed to forget it, am I? All right, then, *Boss*, take over! *I'm* going home!"

"Then you can take Jimmy with you—and give him a bath!"

"WHAT?"

Teacher and pupil gaped, equally appalled.

"It will be a lesson in communication," said Mrs Higdon. "For *both* of you!"

Clenching his teeth (and nostrils against a protesting wave of stench), Tom bore Jimmy away. Annie suppressed a grin. Her years of teaching had taught her a thing or two about how to handle boys—big *and* small. "As for you, Sam," she said sternly, "you may stay behind tonight and scrub away every last speck of pig's blood from the schoolroom floor."

"But there wasn't really a pig," wailed Sam.

"No? And you had convinced us all that there was. Perhaps by the end of the day you'll know the difference between fact and fiction . . . Dora! Call everyone in for current affairs."

This was Mrs Higdon's favourite lesson. She wanted her pupils to see Burston as a part of the whole world and not just a world in itself which most of them would never leave.

"But nobody outside cares about *us*," grumbled Mabel as they lugged in the gramophone. "So why should we care about *them*?"

"Because one day you may have to!" retorted Mrs Higdon, whose sharp ears would have picked up the snore of a flea if it had dared to doze off in one of her classes. "Besides, our little community works in just the same way as a great big one. Take a war, for example. Vast countries or next-door neighbours . . . Is there really so much difference?"

"But we're never going to have a war in Burston!"

"Let's hope not! Now—who's brought in today's newspaper cutting?"

They settled round a fire heaped high with coal and sending out a rich oily perfume from scraps of orange peel singeing among the chunks, and looked at what Emily had found—an item about a lady called a Suffragette who had killed herself by running under the King's horse on Derby Day.

"Who knows what a Suffragette is?" asked Mrs Higdon.

"Do they want votes for women, Madam?" called out Marjory.

"Correct! Why are you laughing, Billy?"

"Because women don't *do* anything. They just stay at home."

"I see. Well, I'd better get back there at once, then!"

Everyone tittered and Billy looked embarrassed. "It's

different for you, Governess. You haven't got any children. You look after us instead. Women look after children. Men look after grown-ups."

"Madam!" Violet's hand shot up. "Queen Victoria ruled for ages, *and* had children. And my Mum goes to work and looks after us *and* manages the money. And if men aren't brought up right when they're little, how will they know what to do when they're big?"

"Yes, but is it worth *dying* for?" Everyone looked round. Dora bit her lip and wished she hadn't spoken. Too late now. "I mean — how far do you have to go when you know you're right?"

"As far as you dare," said Mrs Higdon. "Emily Davison killed herself. I don't suggest we should all do that! But perhaps she felt she had to be a big thing to make up for all those people who did nothing at all. And isn't it monstrous that half of the population of this country has absolutely no say in how it's run?"

"Excuse me . . . "

Mrs Higdon looked round at the sober, top-hatted gentleman who had been listening for some minutes without drawing attention to himself. He removed his hat.

"The name is Ikin. Assistant General to the Norfolk Education Committee. Might I have a word — in *private* ?"

"Of course. Carry on, children." She drew her surprise visitor into a side room. "How may I assist you, Mr Ikin?"

His answer was a blunt question: "What is wrong between you and the Managers?"

"I'm not aware of any problem," replied the mistress coolly.

"Then I regret to inform you that they have written to the Committee saying that they find it impossible to work with you, that you persistently light the school fire — contrary to instructions — and that as you have so many faults to find with the place, would we kindly remove you to a sphere . . . more *genial*?"

"Balderdash!" said Mrs Higdon, and Ikin ducked involuntarily as if the word were a fist aimed at his jaw. "Eland himself said I might light fires when necessary. As for requesting repairs to the roof, the drains and the rancid water pump — since when are these hanging offences?"

Ikin rallied. "What about closing the school without permission?"

"When did I —? Good gracious, man! There was an epidemic of whooping cough! Mr Eland was in Switzerland at the time — "

"It is also felt that you're teaching too many subjects," interrupted Ikin. "I mean to say — when will *village* children ever need to speak *French* ?" He gave a pitying smile.

"It exercises the brain. They do *have* brains, you know!"

"But French history," he countered, wavering. "The *Revolution* ? Don't you think that — "

"That they might get ideas above their station? You want me to teach them their place, so they won't threaten yours!" Her eyes burned him like hot tongs. "I know what all this is about! They're trying to get at Tom because he made them look idiots at the Parish Council elections, I'll eat my umbrella if they're not! Well, you've had your say, and now, *if* you'll excuse me, I've a job to do. And next time His Holiness the Rector *dares* tell me how to teach, I shall come into church and preach his sermon for him!"

Ikin reeled. "I will convey your sentiments," he stammered, nervously replacing his hat. "And I trust I may reassure the Committee that there will be no more friction between you and the Managers?"

"You may do as you please. Good day!"

Friction indeed, she muttered to herself. I'll give 'em friction. She told Dora to ring the bell, and hurried to the schoolhouse where she found Tom disgruntled, weary, and very wet.

"I gave Wittle some of my clothes to go home in," he said. "And burned his. I'm sorry I lost my temper . . . What's wrong, love? You look as if war had just broken out."

"If I'm not very much mistaken, Tom — It *has*!"

CHAPTER 3

"Can I have a dog for Christmas?" asked Baby.

"We don't want a dog," said Ivy. "Nasty, dirty things, all hair and smells. They're not hygienic, are they, Fred?"

"Well, I don't know," said Dad carefully, trying to steer a middle course. "Most people have one. To keep the rats down."

"We don't have rats." True enough. No rat would have dared put a toenail over Ivy Watson's threshold.

"Apart from Reverend Eland," said Dora. "He's always here."

"Don't be disrespectful. And if you're worried about pests, a cat would do the job far better. A cat is efficient. Decorative. Fastidious." Like you, thought Dora.

"Plenty of space for it to run about," went on Dad thoughtfully, "and I could take it rabbiting maybe..."

He drifted off into a pleasant fantasy of himself in corduroys and knotted scarf striding through the autumn leaves with a gun under his arm and a smart collie trotting at his heels. "But it would be your responsibility, Baby," he added, bringing himself back with an effort, "to brush him and feed him. You mustn't ask for things if you're not prepared to look after them. A dog would be part of the family. You'd have to consider his needs and feelings before your own."

Baby nodded enthusiastically, her seven-year-old brain full of fluffy, wriggling bundles, wet noses and waggy tails, of sticks brought panting back, affectionate licks at bedtime and sad howls at the window when she went off to school.

"We are not having a dog," said Ivy. "And that is that."

But hope is sweet. Baby felt that Dad had made some sort of promise, though she avoided mentioning it openly. If Ivy was in earshot, she'd ask: "How many days to

Christmas?" and he'd smile without saying anything, and Ivy would go on knitting, click clack, click clack.

Privately, Dora wondered how he was going to fix it. She had begun seriously to lose faith in him. He was always trying to please everybody, which usually meant that nobody got what they wanted. Marrying Ivy had been the start of it. He'd done that because *she* wanted it and because it was "best for Dora." Dora called it cowardice. Ivy should have been glad she'd found a man who'd give in to her. Anybody else would have told her where to get off. But she wasn't a bit grateful, just complained that he was easily led, couldn't stick at anything. What she meant was that he only gave in so far. He wasn't capable of becoming the man she really wanted, so she felt cheated.

Dora felt cheated too. All that rubbish about sacrificing himself for her education. Mrs Higdon thought she was making real progress, but her father was always too tired to hear about it. He'd sold everybody short and went around acting like a saint . . .

When she caught herself thinking these things, she told herself she was as bad as Ivy. But just like Ivy, she found it impossible to be grateful to someone who only half did things. She couldn't believe the dog would ever appear. He was just keeping Baby sweet. And he'd hurt her far more in the long run.

One afternoon, Baby wrote a poem in school about the dog. Mrs Ling was very pleased and sent her to get one of the Governess's special stars. Mrs Higdon was so impressed, she read it out to her own class.

"My dog Rascal, he's not a mongrel,
He's not a scoundrel, he's got a pedigree.
When I whistle, here comes Rascal,
He'll come with the mistletoe and the Christmas tree."

Everybody clapped, and Violet gave Dora a big wink. Dora was terribly proud. And terribly worried.

Baby drew the outline of a dog and filled it with cartoons of Rascal chasing rabbits round Dad's feet with the words winding in between. Mrs Higdon cut it out and pinned it up on the wall.

"You must take it to show your family after school," she said.

Dora had to stay behind to rehearse for the carol concert, so Baby ran back alone, clutching the poem like a flag. Ivy was in the kitchen, rolling out pastry with swift, sharp jabs.

"Look what I done in school today, Mum!"

"What I did," said Ivy automatically, eyes on her task. Tenderly, Baby laid the crumpled paper on the table and smoothed it out with her forearm. "See!" she said.

"Very nice." Ivy reached for the flour dredger. "Now take it *off* the table, please." Baby picked it up reluctantly.

"It's a poem," she persisted. "Shall I read it to you?"

"A poem?" Ivy flicked over the pastry in one brisk movement and looked round for the cutter. "Oh, very well, then."

"My dog Rascal—" started Baby.

Ivy put down the cutter.

"Not all that nonsense again." She wiped exasperated hands on her apron and looked at Baby for the first time. "Come along then, let's see."

Baby placed the precious, dog-shaped poem into one of those clean red hands. Ivy scoured it with a single furious glance.

"So you've been going round telling everyone about this silly dog?" Ivy had a habit of asking questions you could only answer "yes" to. Baby nodded and looked at her boots. They were speckled with flour. She lifted a foot and wiped it surreptitiously against the back of her other calf.

"And those awful teachers are abetting you, I suppose?"

Baby didn't know what abetting was, but she nodded again, wiping the other boot.

"Well, I won't be blackmailed," declared Ivy. "So you can go back tomorrow and tell everybody, including your teachers, that all this is just something you made up. Is that clear?"

Baby croaked something. Ivy skewered her with a look.

"I said, is that *clear*?"

When the bell rang next morning, Baby stayed outside, face pressed to the wall, refusing to come in. Mrs Higdon was fetched.

"Come along, dear," she said. "We're all waiting for you to put your lovely picture back on the wall. Have you got it with you?"

"Lost it," said Baby indistinctly, kicking the drainpipe.

"You've lost it? Oh dear." Mrs Higdon took her by the shoulders and turned her round. "You shall make us another."

Baby kicked out again, harder. The mistress winced as the boot connected with her shins, but she held on tight as the child started screaming, her face blistered with tears: "I won't make a picture, I *won't*, you can't make me! Everybody hates it, and I'm not going in there to tell them it was all a lie, please don't make me go in, please, *please*!"

"Oh, my dear." Mrs Higdon clutched her. "My poor dear child..."

Just then, the Rector's wife and daughters pedalled past on their bicycles, backs straighter than the steel hatpins securing their latest plumes, knees chewing furiously up and down beneath layers of skirt and petticoat—like a troupe of iron swans, all elegance above water, and agony below. Mrs Eland tinged her bell imperiously, but to no effect. The swans paddled on, feathers decidedly ruffled. Mrs Higdon continued rocking and soothing the small girl, without so much as a glance at the offended posterior of Mrs Eland, bulging over the saddle like a bun on a fork, as it disappeared down the lane. The cygnets sailed after her.

"Evening, Fred. Pint, is it?"

"No, thanks, Tom. I just nipped in to give you a warning." Dora's Dad glanced nervously round the tap-room. "I've been on Fisher's place all day, and guess who he spent the afternoon with?"

"Eland?" Tom gave a sour chuckle. "What did *he* want?"

"Your blood, I reckon. If they can't get you off the Parish

Council, they're going to get at you some way through the school."

"They've started already." Tom told him about Ikin.

"The thing is," said Fred awkwardly. "You know how I'm fixed . . . If it comes to a battle — well, I can't stand by you. Not openly." He paused, unable to meet the teacher's eye.

"Smoke?" Tom proffered his tobacco tin. Fred pulled out his own pipe and stuffed it gratefully. The teacher grinned. "Missus keeps you on short rations, does she?"

In the glow of a match they shared a gleam of understanding.

"Ivy doesn't stop me smoking — but she doesn't like it." He circled the match round the top of the bowl. Tom watched him.

"How's the sketching? I hear you're a bit of an artist."

Fred stifled a curse, dropping the match as it burned his fingers. "Bit of an artist! That's about the size of it." His voice was rough with bitterness. "A bit. But not enough."

They smoked in silence for a moment. Then Tom said, "You're a good man, Fred, and loyal in your own way. But can I offer a word of advice — about this dog. If you're *not* going to get her one, better tell her soon. Christmas is nearly on us."

The stem of Fred's pipe squeaked as his teeth clenched on it hard, but his answer was mild enough, almost humble.

"Fair enough, Tom. Be seeing you."

CHAPTER 4

"Of course, what we *really* need," said Mrs Eland, finishing off her row of embroidery and biting the thread through with the relish of a fox severing the jugular of a small nocturnal animal, "is a nice juicy scandal." She didn't mean a word of it, but these meetings of the School Managers did get so *dreadfully* boring . . .

The assembled gentlemen looked shocked. Then hopeful. Then, glancing at each other, hastily shocked again.

"The very idea! Governess is completely above such a thing."

Mrs Eland nodded, selecting a new thread from her work basket and sucking the tip of it smooth. "And far too old," she murmured, as she held up her needle and squinted through its eye as if measuring it for the passage of a large camel.

"Far too old," agreed Fisher. "Worse luck!"

"I suggest we change the subject immediately," rapped Eland, scowling at his wife.

"Just a thought, dear," she replied demurely, her needle poised. "But you're quite right. You'll never catch either of them out. They're both far . . . too . . ." the needle stabbed, " . . . *good*."

And then a real scandal, big and pink and squelchy, dropped right into the Reverend's lap like a poisoned blancmange.

On a morning in December, when everybody was busy making Christmas cards, the Headmistress felt a tug at her sleeve. She looked up. A shadow of distaste flitted over her sunny features.

"Yes, Gladys? What is it?"

"Letter frob our Mub," said Gladys, a dour eight year

old, dull of eye and dingy skinned. She held out a grubby envelope.

"Handkerchief, dear," said Mrs Higdon, averting her eyes from the gleaming ridge of snot silvering the child's upper lip. Gladys didn't have a hanky. She closed her mouth and sucked hard through both nostrils. Two squirming oysters of snot vanished upwards. Mrs Higdon shuddered.

"From your mother? You mean Mrs Philpot?" Gladys nodded. She was a Barnardo's child who had recently gone to be fostered, and had only been in school a couple of days. Looking at Mrs Philpot's other charge, nine-year-old Ethel, a known liar and troublemaker, the mistress feared for Gladys.

Sighing, Mrs Higdon opened the letter and scanned its contents. Then she put on her spectacles and read it through again slowly. She bit her lip, frowning, and looked over her glasses at the small girl.

"Gladys, do you know what is written here?"

"Yes, Miss."

"You realize that this is a very serious accusation?"

"Yes, Miss," simpered Gladys, suddenly aware that every eye in the room was upon her. She dropped her head selfconsciously and peeped at Ethel Cummings through her eyelashes. Ethel was smirking. The Headmistress gave both of them a long hard look.

"And is it true?" she asked very quietly. Gladys nodded. "Are you quite sure?" Another nod, not so confident this time. The back of her neck started to glow a dull red through the dirt.

"I see." Mrs Higdon's voice was still very gentle, very even. "Mr Higdon, come here a moment, please."

Tom came up. Mrs Higdon took off her glasses. "Now, stand up straight, Gladys, and point out to us the boy whom you say did these rude things in the school playground." So gentle her voice, but every word as clear as cold water. The morning seemed to hold its breath. Pencils and crayons were still. Scissors were silent. A paintbrush tinkled against the side of a jam-jar, then stopped.

"Take your time, dear," said Mrs Higdon. "If any boy here has committed an offence of this nature, he will have to be most severely punished. So I wouldn't want you to make a mistake."

The dull eyes rolled round. Whenever they stopped, the hairs on the back of someone's neck frizzled with fear. When they moved past, there was an audible gulp of relief. Suddenly Gladys swung back, stuck out a skinny arm and pointed.

"Him, Miss! It was 'im!"

"Billy?" said Mrs Higdon. "You mean Billy?"

"Yes, Miss!" Gladys glared at the boy who shrivelled down into his place as if someone had thrown a pan of hot urine over him.

"I see. Violet! Fetch the register." Violet broke out of her trance of terror and hurried to obey. Mrs Higdon opened the book. Her fingers moved down the copperplate row of names and stopped, tapping once. She looked back at Gladys and her mouth widened in an encouraging smile. Gladys grinned back.

"Then how do you explain the fact that on the day in which this rude conduct supposedly occurred, Billy — " she paused, while Billy's face went the colour of a flowerpot and then no colour at all " — was *absent* ?"

Gladys blinked, her grin fading.

"Did you understand the question?"

A hunted animal look came into the girl's eyes. She goggled beseechingly at Ethel, who put a hand over her mouth and pinched her smirk into it.

"It wasn't Billy, was it?"

Gladys pushed her lips together and her cheeks wobbled. She shook her head and a tear fell out of one eye.

"Who was it, then?"

"It was . . ." Water started to run out of the girl's nose, making snail trails through the grime. "It was a boy at my other school. Afore I come here," she snivelled. Mrs Higdon touched her lightly on the shoulder, and the girl flinched.

"Why did you tell this story, if it wasn't true?"

"It was Mum!" blubbered Gladys. "She said she'd tin me if I didn't—"

"Shut it!" screeched Ethel, jumping up. "Shut it! She never! You'll get us *both* . . . It was her idea, Miss, all her idea!"

"Violet—take these girls for a drink of water," said the Headmistress. "Dora, run and fetch Mrs Philpot. And Billy's mother too—Don't be afraid, Billy, I just want her to see you cleared. Everybody else—get on with your work."

Billy's mum arrived in a terrible flap, convinced her son was about to have his tripes torn out and made into bootlaces. Tom barely had time to settle her down on a chair in front of the class before Mrs Philpot blew in as red and ruffled as a flannel petticoat and spoiling for a fight.

"So, Mrs High and Mighty Higdon! What you got to say about this lot, then? Your school's not safe for decent girls, and you're to blame with your fancy ideas. Wait till I tell Rector!"

"If he doesn't know already," Violet muttered to Dora.

"Quiet please!" ordered Mrs Higdon. "Take a seat, Mrs Philpot. Violet, bring in Gladys and Ethel."

Mrs Philpot rustled herself down opposite Billy's mum, legs apart and hands on knees. When the girls came back in, the sight of two angry mothers, facing each other like a pair of firedogs with Mrs Higdon in between, finished them off completely.

"It wasn't me!" roared Gladys. "It was Ethel!"

"No it wasn't! It was Gladys! Parson told her—"

Mrs Philpot jumped up, face mottling with rage, grabbed the girls by the scruffs of their necks and shook them like dusters till they were too dizzy to squeak.

"Perhaps you'd care to retract your earlier remarks," said Mrs Higdon, "now that these two girls, supposedly in your care, have just proved themselves bare-faced liars. It is *their* corrupting influence which is a hazard to all decent children."

"You evil woman!" screamed Mrs Philpot as she hauled the miscreants from the room. "You've twisted everything."

I'll tell Rector how you bullied them into telling lies in front of the whole class!"

The door crashed shut, and the girls were heard howling as she dragged them across the playground, uttering dire threats about what would happen to them when she got them home.

That afternoon, Eland arrived during Tom's Algebra lesson. He did not deign to enter the classroom, but hovered at the door, a thin smile pleating the sides of his thin mouth.

"Governess not here?" he enquired, almost affably.

"She's taken the girls on a nature ramble," Tom replied.

"I see." The Rector's eyes flicked round the room. Billy, still unsure of his safety, recoiled, as if expecting a long sticky tongue to lash out and snatch him up. "Shall we step outside?" suggested Eland cordially, turning back to Tom.

"If it's this business of the Barnardo's girls," said Higdon as the door closed behind them. "It was all cleared up this morning." He summarized events in a couple of pithy sentences.

"All well and good, yes," smiled the Rector. "But was it really necessary for your wife to cane these very small children so savagely that they are now afraid to come back to school?"

"*Cane them?*" Tom was horrified. "Nobody caned 'em. Mrs Higdon doesn't hold with it."

"How curious," purred the Rector. "I have just left the Philpot home, where Gladys and Ethel were in a highly distressed, even hysterical condition." He was still smiling, but there was an air of suppressed danger about him, as strong as the smell of gunpowder. "The younger child's back is cut to the bone, and both girls have severe bruising about the face and arms."

"I'll write to Barnardo's," said Tom grimly, "and tell them."

"I wouldn't advise it. Both girls assert that their injuries were inflicted by Mrs *Higdon*. They claim that she beat them mercilessly to extract a false confession, then forced them to humilate themselves and their innocent stepmother in front of the whole school."

"In front of the whole school is right," said Tom. "Just remember that." He looked witheringly at Eland. "You don't believe a word of that claptrap, any more than I do. Everyone heard them say that Mrs Philpot threatened them in the first place, and sixty pupils saw them leave here without a mark on them. So they must have been thrashed when they got home." (And I wonder who rolled up his sleeves and gave her a hand? he asked himself darkly.) "You'd better come back when Governess returns with the senior girls. They'll corroborate what I've said."

"No one will be more relieved than I," leered the Rector, "to see your wife completely exonerated." And off he went, grinning like a skull. He did not return to hear Mrs Higdon's account.

Soon after, school closed for the holidays. On the last afternoon there was a party. Father Christmas arrived (looking remarkably like Tom Higdon in a false beard) and distributed presents from under the laden tree. Mrs Higdon discreetly slipped coins wrapped in coloured paper to the poorest children.

Jimmy Wittle got two coins, new trousers, boots, a drawing book and a bright green pencil. He didn't smell any more because Governess had him to tea once a week with his mum, and made sure he had a bath between the bread and butter and the cake. And she talked to them. His mum said hardly anything — a lost cause — and Jimmy said little at first, for he was holding on hard to his surliness, but each time he said a little more. And when he couldn't think what to say, she let him draw it. His pictures were pinned up on the wall, and the children encouraged to ask him about them. A slow process, but it was working.

School finished early because it looked like snow — and because Mrs Higdon knew that, no matter how much fun it is, the best bit of the last day of term is the bit just after it's finished.

CHAPTER 5

On Saturday Ivy took the girls shopping in Diss. It was piercingly cold, but the narrow streets were bright with sunshine and the frosted cobblestones glittered like fish scales. Ivy stopped for a moment to gaze at her favourite row of smart Georgian houses, smugly dusted with sparkling face powder, then puffed out a cloud of crystallized envy and led the way up the slippery hill into the market.

"Fancy a nice bird?" came a jeering cry. It was George Durbidge. Tilting her chin, Ivy hustled the girls past his stall.

"Drunk!" she sniffed. "And at *this* hour of the day!"

Dora craned back to stare at the mistletoe swagged booth in which Durbidge strutted as solo actor, his face a luminous mask of jollity in the harsh incandescent flares which blazed on leaf and berry. From a pelmet of leaves, unnaturally green and full of spiteful white pips, hung a row of evil hooks spiked through the necks of pheasants and the black, leaf-shaped feet of very dead ducks. Their bodies looked like a row of pump bags hanging from pegs in the school cloakroom. Rubbery dead fish gaped up from the slab beneath. Ivy yanked her back into line.

"Poached, every one of them, I'll be bound!"

They spent the next hour more agreeably, munching chestnuts, eye wateringly hot from a soot-caked brazier, picking out oranges from nests of straw, sighing over frozen flowers and tinsel cherubs and a million different colours of sherbert spooned out into twists of paper . . . Then Baby started to grizzle.

"I'm cold!" she whined, stomping her feet on the pavement, "and I want my dinner!"

"Too early for dinner, you'll be sick," said Ivy. "Let's look at the decorations in the church. The Vicar's charming."

"Don't let Eland find out. He'll be jealous."

"What was that, Dora?" Ivy harpooned her with a smile.

Dora wriggled. "I said I'd rather buy some presents. In *secret*."

"Oh." Ivy looked contrite. "Well, you'd better have some money, then." Holding her handbag close to her stomach, she opened the purse inside without taking it out, so no one could see. "Here. Take this. And don't talk to any strange men."

The market was glorious without Ivy pulling forward and Baby dragging back. Dora wandered about in a delicious haze, unable to choose between so many delights. The jumble stall was the best — piled high with rags, old picture frames, the flightless wings of bright and broken fans, bits of cheap jewellery, tasteless but tantalizing. There was even a yellowing bridal gown hanging from a nail which had bled rust across the bodice.

And then she saw it. And the rest of the world vanished.

It was a statuette, not three inches high, of a horse. A miniature horse spun out of glass and sunshine. Dainty and proud, high stepping on four slender legs, it seemed poised to take off and canter on the air. Every line of it quivered with light, from the reckless sweep of the mane to the tips of the four tattooing hooves, as tiny and sharp as sparks. It was the single most perfect, most exquisite thing she had ever seen. She moved a dreaming hand to touch . . .

"You want to buy?"

She looked up. And up. The woman behind the stall seemed higher than a house, tall and sooty as a factory chimney. Smoke gusted out from between teeth clamped round a clay pipe; black hair billowed from under a man's tweed hat.

"You like the leetle 'orse, yes?" prompted the woman in a voice like a tune played on Mrs Higdon's gramophone with a blunt needle. Dora nodded. The woman grinned. "To you . . . Seexpence!"

Sixpence! It was all she had left. It was as much as a boy could earn in a whole day picking stones out of the fields. But she wanted the horse — oh, how she wanted it! It was like a pain inside. Her hand slid into her pocket . . .

"Come away from there this minute!"

Ivy. Rigid as ice, only the trembling grapes on her new hat betraying the emotions churning underneath it. She seized Dora's arm in a grip that would have throttled a goose and hauled her away. "I told you not to speak to strange men!"

"It's not a man!"

"The next worst thing. A gipsy!" She pulverized the word as if punishing it for daring to squeeze past her lips. "I can't believe it — you were talking, actually *talking* to that Dreadful Creature!"

Dora could feel her shaking. It's not anger, she thought, it's fear. Of a battered old gipsy woman. Because she's wild and different and dares to be dirty and free.

"I only asked the price," she said sulkily.

"Price? Of what? You haven't bought anything have you?"

"The little horse," faltered Dora, feeling self pity starting to fill up her face and spill out of eyes and nose. "And I didn't buy it. But, oh!" — a wail of naked despair — "It was so beautiful!"

"What's the matter with Dora?" asked Baby, her voice getting the crumpled sound of imminent and sympathetic sobs.

"Nothing at all," came the crisp reply. "She's just hungry. A nice cup of tea and we'll all feel better."

Within seconds of their arrival, Auntie Win's best copper kettle was on the hob, and she was regaling them with its by now ancient history. "It was one of many prizes," she told Baby, who was busy eating seed cake, "but Wally always said it was his favourite . . . "

Sepia and long deceased, Uncle Wally stared mournfully from a dozen framed photographs. He'd been big in cotton somewhere in Lancashire and grown monster gooseberries in his spare time. Baby looked impressed and reached for the crumpets.

Dora sat stiffly silent in the hard-backed chair, crumbling a single biscuit on to the willow patterned plate. "I should have known I couldn't have it," she was thinking. "But at least I *know*. Baby will never forgive Dad if she doesn't get that dog..."

The following day Mrs Higdon received a summons from the School Managers to attend an Inquiry into the Philpot Affair.

"I'll send a doctor's note," she said. "This cough has gone to my chest, and if I have to spend an evening with that man, I'll only come back with a pain in the neck on top of everything else."

"I think you'd better go, all the same," warned Tom. Then wished he hadn't. Strong drink, dead flesh, and friendly advice were the three things his wife had sworn never to take.

Not surprisingly, the Managers, in her absence, found that there were "good grounds" for Mrs Philpot's complaints. The clerk duly sent instructions that Ethel and Gladys were to be readmitted after Christmas and not victimized in any way.

"The cheek of it!" exploded Annie. "We know who's being victimized. And if this is the end of the matter, I'll eat my—"

Tom looked at her ancient umbrella poking out of a cracked plant pot along with assorted rulers, walking sticks, and a selection of dried ferns.

"Shall I pass you the salt?" he said.

CHAPTER 6

It was Christmas Eve, the night of the carol concert. Dad was there, together with all the other proud fathers who had been banned from their family kitchens. Eland and the Managers sat through the whole thing with faces like cold custard. All went well, however, until Dora got up for her solo.

Dad had obviously taken a fortifying nip beforehand because he started applauding before she even opened her mouth, then stopped himself and looked round sheepishly. Worse was to come. Dora had two verses of "Silent Night", and he got up and started applauding *again* as soon as she'd finished the first one. This time everyone laughed, and the Elands swapped pitying glances as Dad was pulled down with a bump and shushed by Harry Ellis. Dora went hot all over and wished she could melt and run down through a crack in the floorboards.

Herbert Garnham was next. His father stood at the back, white beard jutting above his collar like a frozen waterspout, his wife beside him—a homely, female version of Bob Ford, who was of course her brother. Ford's chins joggled with pride as his nephew sang "Silent Night" in a beautiful, pure tenor. The whole audience were moved by his youth and simplicity. Then Baby came on and Dad started pointing and grinning.

Dora was mortified. She told herself it shouldn't matter because most of the dads were carrying on in the same way. But it *did* matter. He was her Dad, he was Special, he was on show and he was letting himself down. Baby did a dance with some of the other infants dressed as Christmas elves, and Dad actually *wept*. He gave a sob loud enough for everyone to hear. It was horrendous.

When it was all over, he rushed up to them and lifted Dora off the ground in the kind of hug that was all very well at home (and which she didn't get enough of these days) but was unbelievably embarrassing in front of everybody else. "My little girl!" he kept saying adoringly over her head to anyone within range, while Dora went stiff with humiliation.

"Put me *down*, Dad!" she hissed. "Nobody's interested."

He released her and looked hopefully at Baby. She was loyal. She came up and hugged his legs in front of them all. Then she smiled up at his beaming, foolish face and said for the whole village to hear: "Is my doggie coming tomorrow?"

"We'd better get home," said Dora quickly. "Coming, Dad?"

"Er — not yet." He looked like a schoolboy caught with a frog in his pocket. "Got to have a quick one with the blokes. Celebrate having two brilliant daughters!" He bent to embrace Dora but she stepped firmly aside.

"See you later, then." And she marched Baby away, leaving him standing there, arms dangling, like a scarecrow with all the supports pulled out.

Ivy was in festive mood, having tackled her chores. She produced hot mince pies, let the girls stay up an extra hour, and actually *listened* to all they had to tell about the concert, though Dora edited events to present Dad in the best light.

Later, when she was half asleep, Dora thought she heard him come in, then raised voices:

"How *could* you, Fred? What possessed you?"

"What's wrong with it? It's got as much right to live as anything else." Dad's voice lifted in angry self-justification.

"Be quiet, Fred, you'll wake the children. What kind of Christmas d'you think this is going to be *now*?"

Dora couldn't hear any more. She drifted off to sleep and when she awoke, it was Christmas Day. She sat up with an obscure feeling of dread. At the bottom of the bed was the stocking she had hung up empty the night before, now full of magical bumps and bunions. She drew it towards her mechanically and started to take out the contents.

First was an orange wrapped in shiny paper. She smoothed out the creases and put it aside carefully. Then a knobbly package — newspaper this time — the best stuff was always saved for the boring presents. She felt round it, playing the Christmas and birthday game of teasing herself, which was normally such fun, but felt this time vaguely unreal. It was a different *kind* of teasing — this pretence that Christmas was going to be all right when she knew something was about to go horribly wrong. Her fingers located four spikes, and her heart gave a sudden jolt — it *couldn't* be!

She tore off the wrapping, and there it was. Skipping and glittering in the palm of her hand, a miracle of delicacy and disdain, the filigree glass pony from the market stall.

She ran a wondering finger over each of the extravagantly slender legs, pressed the tiny, sharp hooves against the cushion of her thumb one after another, and prickled with wonder. Tied to one of its impossibly thin fetlocks was a minute gift tag with "Merry Christmas" written on it. "Merry Christmas — from Ivy."

Dora placed the pony on the bedside table. In the candle light it glistened as if it had been carved from an icicle. Her joy in its possession mingled with a strange, heavier kind of joy almost like guilt — that Ivy, who had made no promises, had remembered, realized what it meant to her, summoned up all her courage to face "that Dreadful Creature" the gipsy woman. While Dad made promises all the time and, that's all they were. Promises.

Baby woke up and started on *her* stocking. She pulled out nuts, sweets, hankies, a miniature needle case, a twist of sewing silk, blue enough almost to taste, and four lead pencils, so new they looked the same at both ends because they hadn't been sharpened yet, and made your teeth simply ache to bite them. Dora knew where *they* had come from. Out of Dad's workbox.

Baby shook the stocking to be absolutely sure that there was nothing else. Dora guessed what she was looking for — a rubber bone or a collar, some clue to a canine presence. There was nothing.

Voices downstairs again. A quarrel flaring up and being damped down. Then footsteps ascending and a tap on the door.

"Merry Christmas!" There was a brightness in Ivy's voice, the kind of brightness you get when you've worked and worked to get a shine out of something that wants to stay dull and dusty.

"Is my doggie downstairs?" asked Baby, without any real hope. There was a silence on the other side of the door. Then Dad's voice came up from below, sounding defiantly cheerful.

"Yes!" he shouted.

Baby's mouth dropped open just long enough for her to fill her lungs. She let out a whoop of joy — "Rascal!" — threw open the door and hurtled downstairs in her nightie. Dora hurried after her, still with that queer feeling of dread. Baby landed at the bottom with an ecstatic bump.

"Just a moment." Ivy put out a restraining arm. She was looking at something. On top of the kitchen table stood an old crate, half covered by a bit of blanket. Something inside was making squeaks and catarrhal snufflings like a drunk old man. The warm room already smelled distinctively of dog.

"Is that Rascal?" whispered Baby. Ivy put her arm round the small girl and drew her close in to an aproned hip.

"Listen, dear," she said. "Rascal isn't..."

"Isn't he in there?" Baby's mouth widened, ready to howl.

"Yes, dear, he's there." Ivy glared at Dad as if to say, Why don't you *help*? "It's just that he may not be all you expected... But you're big enough to take a bit of disappointment, aren't you?"

"Disappointment, nothing," said Dad, angry and blustering. "She's no business being disappointed. She's a kid, he's a dog. They'll love each other and that's all there is to it."

Ivy flashed him a look. *Such* a look. Dora thought it must go through him like a flame through paper. A breath of wind would dissolve him into charred fragments. But he held his ground. Just seemed to curl up slightly at the corners.

"Let the child decide for herself," he said.

Ivy's eyes reached for Dora's. In them Dora read something she had never seen before. It was a plea for help.

"Shall I look first?" she asked. Ivy nodded.

"*Don't gang up on me.*"

Dad was out of his chair, really angry now. "Come on, Baby, come and see your blasted puppy. You wanted a dog, and I've got you one. And I hope you're *all* satisfied!"

Baby broke free and ran forward. Dora moved simultaneously, but too late. Baby was up on the kitchen stool, pulling back the blanket, parting the straw, peering jubilantly inside.

And then she started screaming.

Dora had never seen anyone move so fast as Ivy did then. She whisked up Baby as a whirlwind whisks up small animals in its path, and deposited her in the next room with a furious hiss at Dad: "Happy now?" The door banged behind them.

Dad sat down heavily and looked at his hands. Big, stupid hands, raw and clumsy, dangling guiltily in his lap from the improbably narrow cuffs of his Sunday jacket. Dora found herself wondering how he could ever have squeezed such hands through the sleeves. They fell open helplessly and he jerked his head towards the crate. "See for yourself," he said.

Dora went over and lifted the blanket.

The shock was like iodine poured into an open cut. Bald and pink and slimy, with a few tufts of gingerish hair, the creature inside looked as if it had been born too early — or shouldn't have been born at all . . .

But Dora reached in and touched it, and felt the warmth of its body — and she was done for. She lifted it out gently. A tiny heart was ticking madly underneath her fingers, and the stumpy legs made feeble kicking movements. Its head, lolling against her hand, looked squashed as if someone had picked it up in a pair of nutcrackers — one eye was pinched permanently shut and it only had one ear. The other was just a shred. But the good eye, bleary and blue, seemed to be trying to focus on Dora, and a scrap of pink tongue flickered out and licked her finger. She shivered with delight. And then started to cry.

"Oh, Dad," she said. "How could you?"

"You sound just like Ivy. Always putting me in the wrong."

"But what if you *are* wrong, Dad? Are we supposed to say you're right?" *We*, she thought sorrowfully. He's right, we *are* ganging up on him.

Ivy came back in, closing the door tightly behind her. She glared at her husband, her face whiter than starch.

"Tell me," she said in a voice so cold it could have cracked open a tombstone. "Did you do it to spite me? Was *that* it?"

"I don't know what you mean," mumbled Dad.

"You had to prove you could do it, didn't you? Even at the expense of your own child. And don't say you were sorry for that thing — you haven't done it any favours." Her eyes raked the animal with loathing. "Well, they say it's better to give than to receive, and you've certainly proved that today. I bet you're *really* proud of yourself, and to Hell with anybody else's feelings!"

Dora had never heard her swear. It was terrifying to see her so nearly out of control. Dad had the grace to look shamefaced.

"I didn't mean any harm. It seemed like the right thing — Look, it's not so bad, is it?" He turned beseeching eyes on Dora as she cuddled the "it" in question.

"Not so bad!" Ivy's hands clenched at her sides as if she were physically holding down her temper like a petticoat in a gale. There was so much acid in her voice it could have stripped the enamel off her teeth. "It's a monster! Its own mother would have eaten it, given the chance, that's nature's way. You and your stupid pals . . ." Temper and voice were rising in spite of her efforts.

"Or maybe *not* so stupid. Oh, I can guess what Bill thought: Get rid of it on Fred, he's fool enough to buy anything. Well, you had no right. No right to force it to live, and no right — "

Her hands flew up and clutched at her throat as if she felt

a scream about to burst out of it. "No right to inflict it on that poor child in there!"

But he wasn't listening. He was staring at the door opening behind her and Baby emerging, very pale with pink eyes. She fixed them on Dad and said, in a flat voice coagulated with stale tears, "It's all right. I know it's my fault."

"But it *isn't*," said Ivy, appalled.

Dad gazed at his littlest child, near to tears himself.

"You don't mind?" he whispered. She shook her head.

"You said you'd get me a dog, and you did."

"That isn't a dog!" protested Ivy. "It's a *thing*!"

"I'll feed it and brush it and take it for walks," went on Baby stoically. "I said I would. And I will." Her speech finished, she turned to go. But Dad hadn't understood.

"Don't you want to come and stroke him?" he said. She didn't move. "Come on, Baby," he urged. "I know you're really going to love each other."

She lifted her head and looked straight at him.

"I promised to feed it and brush it and walk it. I didn't promise to love it. And don't call me Baby any more, please." Then she turned and went upstairs.

It was a vile Christmas.

CHAPTER 7

It was a *busy* Christmas for Mr Eland, who was filling up a sackful of surprises specially for Mrs Higdon. On 23 January 1914 he sent a detailed letter to the Norwich Education Committee.

The dog grew up fast. He learned how to get about in a waddling run with his bad leg tucked up, but had a habit of bumping into the furniture. "Rascal" was now out of the question as a name, and in the end, Dad chose one, quite by accident.

"You'll never get that mongrel to do tricks," said Ivy brutally one night when she had been watching Dora "training" the puppy for the best part of an hour. "He's plain daft."

"Most geniuses are a bit touched," said Dad consolingly. "Like Van Gogh. Come to think of it, he looks a bit like him!"

"Van Gogh?" asked Dora. "He was a painter, wasn't he?"

"Yes. Gingery haired and eccentric. And blue eyed." Van Gogh (pronounced Goff—which sounded like one of his scratchy barks) it was to be. VG for short.

Dora especially liked the shorter version because it also meant Very Good. Sometimes Mrs Higdon put VG on the bottom of her compositions, which gave her a special thrill, because she had decided that with the teacher's help, she would go on to be a writer of some kind. That was the new Plan. She'd tried to tell Dad about it, but it didn't seem to have sunk in. He'd just smiled and said "Well done!" and gone right back into a sort of daze. Perhaps now he'd stopped painting, he thought stuff like that was all useless . . .

"You've brought my cocoa! Thank you, Violet!"

Gratefully Mrs Higdon put aside the spelling test she was correcting during break. She grasped the mug, inhaling the sweet steam before puckering up for an experimental sip. Her face sagged contentedly. Her eyes closed.

"Governess, is it true the Education people are taking you to court?"

The eyes snapped open.

"News travels fast." Mrs Higdon put down the mug. "No, it is *not* true," she said firmly. Violet gave a sigh of relief and turned to go. "However—" Violet stopped. "There *is* going to be an Inquiry into a number of crimes I am supposed to have committed. But I want everyone to know that *I* requested it in order to clear my name once and for all."

Violet grabbed her courage and held on to it. "Then can Marjory and me come and give evidence?" she asked.

Mrs Higdon stared at her. "*Evidence?*"

"That Gladys said Eland made them tell those lies, and told Mrs Philpot they'd be taken off her and she wouldn't get any more money unless they did."

Mrs Higdon's eyes rested thoughtfully on the earnest young face. "I hope it won't come to that," she said. "Especially since they denied it all afterwards . . . Run along now, dear, and don't worry."

"But, Governess—You know when you had your troubles at Wood Dalling? And you . . . you lost—Why didn't anybody help?"

"They tried," said Mrs Higdon. "They got a petition together, but nobody took any notice of it. So they gave up."

"But they were grown-ups!" protested Violet. "They should have been able to do something!"

"They were afraid," was the bleak reply.

"Well, what's the point of growing up if you're still going to be afraid?" Violet raked back her flop of hair furiously.

The Headmistress gave a sad smile. "Grown-ups call it discretion," she said. "And the older they get, the more things they find to be afraid of—the more things they think they stand to lose . . ."

"But you're not afraid, are you, Madam?"

Mrs Higdon brisked herself together. "Not when I'm right!"

"Then neither," said Violet Potter, "am *I*!"

"Who's that?" asked Marjory as she and Violet were bowling one hoop between them past the schoolhouse on a day early in February. Violet stopped, steadying the hoop expertly with the tip of her stick, and examined the gentleman in frock coat and spats who was being admitted to the Higdons' parlour.

"The man from NUT," she said knowledgeably. "National Union of Teachers, to you. Wonder what *he*'s got to say for himself?"

"The Union wishes to make it clear, Mrs Higdon," the man from NUT was explaining, "that since this is the *second* time you've quarrelled with your Managers — need I mention Wood Dalling? — this Inquiry can only proceed at your own risk."

Tom thumped the table. "Risk of what? Another transfer? Well, I'm blowed if I'll let them get away with it twice!"

"With respect," interrupted their guest, a Mr Peggram, "no allegations have been made against *you*, Mr Higdon—"

"Are you a complete fool? If they dismiss Annie, I have to go too. It's *me* they're after, for being a union man and for setting the Parish Council to rights. That's what's behind it all — just like at Wood Dalling!"

"Well, if you honestly think that was the case at Wood Dalling, wasn't it rather rash to repeat the experiment here?"

"How else were we to put the record straight?" Annie spoke up for the first time. "And prove that we won't be tyrannized?"

"The fact remains, Headmistress, that the charges

against you have nothing to do with local politics and everything to do with your apparent inability to get on with the School Managers. Now, I've drafted a letter for you to send to the Education Committee which I'm sure will settle the matter amicably."

Annie read it through silently and handed it back.

"You want me to lie? This letter says that I did not punish the Barnardo girls *excessively*. I didn't punish them at all!"

Peggram pinched the skin at the top of his nose and screwed up his eyes. He was developing a seismic headache.

"This Inquiry can do you nothing but harm. Why not temporize, be friendly to the Managers, climb down a little — "

"Climb down!" barked the mistress, bristling like a terrier. "And let that sickly little toad Eland walk all over us?"

"Very well, very well!" Peggram took a step back as if afraid she might savage his trouser leg. "We'll put our trust in the Committee . . . "

"Who also happen to be landowners," interjected Tom.

"Possibly. But if you present your case calmly and without bias, we may hope for a satisfactory conclusion." He made a dart for the door. "Good day to you, then — And keep smiling on the Managers!"

Marjory whacked the hoop and it jiggered off, bouncing and skimming through the dirt. They saw it reach the corner of the lane, tilt over to take the curve, then vanish. Marjory belted after it, and came to an abrupt halt outside Blossom Cottage.

"Where's it g — "

She bit off the end of the question as a skinny black arm unfurled itself from behind the hedge and a cold white hand gripped her shoulder.

"Marjory, dear!" The Reverend's lips writhed in a horrible parody of a smile. "What a fortunate meeting!"

"What d'*you* want?" muttered Marjory, trying to wriggle away. His fingers were as strong as pliers.

"A quiet word—about the Inquiry." The pale lips stretched wider, uncovering little rat's teeth. "I trust you will be attending to give evidence."

"What evidence?" Marjory twisted round. Where was *Violet*?

"Why, that you saw and heard Billy's rude behaviour in the playground last year. You did, didn't you?"

"No, I didn't." The fingers squeezed tighter. "Ow! Stop it!"

"You're an ungrateful little girl, Marjory. I've done a lot for your father in the past . . . " The fingers nipped so hard she thought they would leave holes. "And it's time you paid me back."

"No!" Indignation overcame pain. "My father's never told a lie in his life, and he's not going to let me tell one either!"

Three million volts sizzled through the ends of the white pincers. The world shuddered into a blur. She felt Eland's face close to her own, his breath sticking to her like frostbite. "I could make things very difficult for your father," he whispered. "So don't make things difficult for me . . . "

"That's a wicked, cowardly thing to say!"

Sparkling with fury, Violet grabbed Eland's coat-tails and swung on them. He let go of Marjory and his talons turned into empty rubber gloves, flapping feebly as Violet screamed up at him: "We'll tell everybody what we know! Like who *really* thrashed Gladys and Ethel. You won't get away with it!"

Eland's pale face went paler. "I'll bring an action for slander!" he threatened. "It's your word against mine!" And he pushed roughly past them and headed for the Rectory, trembling with anger.

"What'll we do?" wailed Marjory. "I can't go to the Inquiry *now* !"

"Then *I'll* go," said a soft voice. They whirled round. Dora stepped out from behind the hedge. "I heard what he said just now and I'll swear it in court." They stared at her.

"What about your Auntie Ivy?"

"I won't tell her. Not till after. It'll be all right, Governess is bound to win. In a fair trial."

CHAPTER 8

The NUT provided a King's Counsel for Mrs Higdon, the highly esteemed Mr Henry Lynn. He arrived by motor car — quite an event in Burston — with his clerk, Mr Cooper, who scurried round collecting statements on behalf of the mistress and chirruping "A beautiful case! A beautiful case!" to anyone within hearing.

Mr Lynn advised Tom to stay away from the Inquiry, insisting that it had nothing to do with him as he faced no charges.

"But it's everything to do with me! The farmers — "

"Irrelevant and immaterial. Mrs Higdon's case must be judged on its own merits." And he refused to discuss it further.

On the first afternoon of the Inquiry, a Monday in February, a row of children in best sailor suits of starched zephyr waited by the playground to see the Committee arrive. The noble profiles of the President and his subordinates glided past like yachts before the breeze, then put about and vanished into the school. Governess appeared next with Mr Lynn, followed by Cooper dancing crabwise under a nose-high pile of legal tomes. Last came Eland, sweating like a Stilton inside his finest and most funereal black. The door closed behind him with a disapproving click.

The children squatted down in the dust to wait. Several minutes later, Jimmy Wittle came whistling along, looking as nonchalant as a fellow can who's just had his nits cut out and most of his head shaved. One central tuft remained, giving him the appearance of a bad-tempered coconut.

"What you doin'?" he demanded, though he knew the answer and was as worried about Governess as anybody. They told him.

"What good's that?" He screwed up his face, thinking. Then unscrewed it again. Actions rather than words.

"I'll just shin up the ole pear tree at the back," he said casually. "See what's doing." He vanished behind a hedge and they watched his tuft of hair flit along the top of it, then out of sight. Ten minutes later there was a terrible howl from the rear of the school and the tuft came hurtling back.

"Sexton nabbed me," he complained, rubbing his backside. "Gave me a kick right up the —"

"Never mind that — What were they *saying*?"

Jimmy squirmed his feet inside his new boots. "Well, it were about Governess lighting school fires when she shouldn't."

"But Eland said it was up to her!" protested Violet.

"That was before he made himself Chairman of the Managers," said Dora. "And remember when that was? Right after the Parish Council Elections! *That's* when he started making a fuss about the fires. It's all in my diary." She held it up. "Exhibit One!"

"Oi!" objected Jimmy. "*I'm* talking! Parson said he told the education people about the fires and they ticked off Mrs Higdon, and ever since, she's been rude to him in front of everybody." He stopped, stunned. It was the longest speech he had ever made.

"What's he mean by rude?" asked Emily. Jimmy counted off the points on his spiky fingers: "She never bowed to Miss Eland when she whizzed past on her bike. Didn't answer when Rector said Good Mornin' in the street. And she gave Mrs Eland a cold re — re —"

"Reception?"

"Yeah. When she come to visit. What's that, then, a salad?"

Just then the school door opened and Annie Higdon came out. Tom appeared from nowhere, loping across to seize her hands.

"How did it go?"

"Fine so far." She bestowed a gracious smile upon Eland who, yellow with wrath, was trying to sidle out behind Mr Lynn.

"I think we can dispose of the charge of Firelighting Contrary to Instructions," said the eminent KC loftily. "As for Discourtesy to the Managers — piffling little complaints! The President himself said that they were very slight. Friday's our big day. That's when they'll get out the heavy artillery!"

"What's the heavy artillery?" asked Marjory.

"Chamberpot," was Violet's grim reply.

Mrs Philpot flounced into her chair, yanking Ethel and Gladys down beside her. Friday afternoon, the second day of the Inquiry. Eland looked rather more cheerful — he'd arrived with his own lawyer, Mr Reeves, and Fisher had come along to lend moral support. Mrs Higdon ignored them all, busily making notes on a pad on her knee. The President banged his gavel.

"This afternoon we must consider a most serious charge. A matter of unjust and over-zealous punishment. Firstly, we must establish if the 'rude conduct in the playground' did indeed take place. If it did not, then the Mistress was within her rights to punish the children for lying. Secondly, we must consider if the *level* of punishment was justified."

There was no punishment, Annie pencilled in furiously.

Mr Reeves' first witness, an eighty-year-old woman, mummified with age and respectability, was helped into the stand.

"Rude conduct?" she cackled. "In the playground? Oh, yes! The things I've seen and heard there on my way to church!"

Mrs Higdon tapped her lawyer's knee and hissed, "That woman's had seven illegitimate children! Rude conduct, indeed! What about her own?"

"Mr Lynn — Do you wish to call any witnesses to dispute this lady's claim?" asked the President. Mr Lynn rose.

"I am uncertain as to the validity of calling a witness to testify to something which he did *not* see or hear," he replied in bland tones. And he sat down again.

"I take it that means No," said the President waspishly.

"Very well. Mrs Higdon, would you give us your account of the events which took place in school last December?" Annie did so, plainly and simply.

Eland next took the stand to render at length his own version, adding: "Even after the Managers had acquitted Mrs Philpot of the allegations made by Mrs Higdon — who did not design to attend our hearing — the Headmistress persistently cross-questioned the girls on their return to school, kept them in at playtimes and denied them treats, all in the hope that they would contradict themselves — which they never did, in spite of the appalling punishment she had already inflicted upon them in the previous December."

Mr Lynn was consulting a book. Why doesn't he *object*? fumed Annie. Why doesn't he say that the caning hasn't been proved and can't be used as evidence? Mr Lynn turned a page.

"In my opinion," concluded Eland, "this constant haranguing was most detrimental to the tone and discipline of the school. The woman is impossible, dangerous! I wouldn't care to have her visit my home if my daughter were there, and furthermore — "

"Thank you, Reverend," cut in the President quickly. "Mr Lynn — Do you wish to cross-examine?" Mr Lynn shook his head.

The man's *hopeless*, raged Annie inwardly. Why wouldn't they let me do it myself? I could wipe the floor with this lot.

The President now turned his attention to Mrs Philpot, "I have no wish for your children to suffer any further harrassment than they have undergone already, so I'll keep it brief. If I might just put one or two questions to Ethel?"

"Feel free, Your Honour!" sniggered Mrs Philpot coyly. She gave Ethel a dig in the ribs and the girl jerked upright.

"Thank you," said the President. "Now, Ethel — Can you tell us, in your own words . . . Why did Mrs Higdon cane you?"

"*Object! Object!*" mouthed Annie at Mr Lynn. He put up a restraining hand then leaned on his elbow, fondling his ear lobe while he stared intently at the girl and waited for her answer. It didn't come. The President tried again.

"Was it for saying that the boy was rude to you in the playground?"

He had plopped the words right into her mouth.

"Yes, sir!" she said, gulping with gratitude.

Annie's pencil gouged her pad. "Leading the witness! By her snotty nose!"

She thrust the pad at Mr Lynn who shook his head irritably and pushed it back.

"Thank you, Ethel." The President leaned back, tugging his waistcoat down over a modest paunch. "Now — As regards the suitability of the foster parents — " He inclined his head towards his two colleagues. "I believe you have evidence germane to the case?"

"We have," they said in one voice, rising together like Tweedledum and Tweedledee, and consulting identical notes: "On visiting the Philpot residence we found it to be a most hygienic and suitable accommodation."

Annie jabbed her pencil into Mr Lynn's arm. "Only because Eland moved them into a new place just before the visit," she whispered fiercely. He nodded, and shifted his chair sideways.

"And that's another thing!" Mrs Philpot shouted out unexpectedly, creaking to her feet (she was breaking in a new corset.) "Tom Higdon wrote to Barnardo's to say we lived in a hovel. That's slander! And he said my Ethel was a slate loose!"

"I have the letters here," said Mr Reeve, rising like a wraith and flourishing a sheaf of papers. "It is my intention to offer them as evidence against Mr Higdon."

"Wait a minute!" Annie jumped up. "Tom isn't here to defend himself!" She turned on her KC. "You said he was to stay away!"

"You mean he was too chicken to come!" jeered Mrs Philpot.

The Presidential gavel banged twice.

"I think it appropriate to call a short recess at this point," he said, lancing disapproval at the two ladies as they squared up to each other across the schoolroom. "Ten minutes."

87

"You *must* object," Annie told her lawyer, when order had been restored. "Those letters are inadmissable evidence. Tom isn't being charged, and they can't use them against me."

"It might have been better if they had never been written," murmured the KC. "Barnardo's passed them straight on to Eland, who is of course paymaster to the foster parents. Your husband used language I should find extremely difficult to justify."

"Why? Everything he said was true! And what about Johnnie Philpot — That jailbird's not fit to be a foster-parent!"

"He's paid his debt to society. And keep your voice down, Mrs Higdon — We don't want a slanging match."

While this argument was being conducted inside, Dora and the other children waited outside as before.

"When are they going to call you?" fretted Violet.

"Any time now," said Dora. So they waited . . . And waited . . . Towards five o'clock, Tom joined them, gnawing his pipe and pacing like a pregnant father, pulling on braces and moustache in turn. At half-past five, the school door opened.

"This is it!" Violet gave Dora a hug. "All the best!" But it was a false alarm. People were coming out. Mrs Higdon hurried over and steered Tom aside.

"They're considering the verdict — and it doesn't look good. Mr Lynn didn't put up any fight at all! I think he's afraid to win, in case they have to reopen the file on Wood Dalling. They want rid of us, Tom. We're an embarrassment."

"Don't worry. The only real problem is the Barnardo's business. Win that one, and you're home and dry . . . "

"Hrrrrmph!" Tweedledum and Tweedledee were standing in the porch. "The Inquiry will reconvene — for the Verdict."

Violet and Dora clutched hands. "Good luck, Governess!" yelled Violet.

Mrs Philpot creaked round angrily, her small blackcurrant eyes sour with malice. "I'm not dead yet!" she shouted savagely. "I'm not dead yet!" And she let out a wheezing laugh, like somebody sawing through a brick. Eland hastily escorted her inside. Tom took Annie's arm.

"I'm coming in with you," he said. "They can't object."

Inside the courtroom it was noisier than the Crown Inn on a Friday night. The President's gavel nailed down a silence over the proceedings. He lifted a sheet of paper and read from it.

"The findings of this Inquiry into the allegations against Mrs Anne Katherine Higdon are as follows — Regarding the alleged Discourtesy to the Managers — " He paused, as if unable to read his writing, and all eyes turned towards Annie. She scribbled on her pad "No problem with this one," and pushed it across to Tom.

"We find the charge — proven."

Annie went white. "But he said himself on Monday that the discourtesy was nothing!" Tom grabbed the pencil and wrote, "Don't worry — it's not the big one." She bit her lip and looked round for Mr Lynn, who, seated at a safe distance, was flicking through a book with magnificent unconcern.

The President returned to his papers. "With regard to the Barnardo's children . . . "

Annie's hand found and clung on to Tom's. Eland sat up straight in his chair, the bones in his spine making tiny popping noises. Fisher's Adam's apple started jumping up and down, rasping itself raw against his collar.

"We find no evidence that the girl Ethel Cummings is mentally or morally deficient as stated in the letters of the Headteacher and her husband — which were not warranted by the facts of the case."

"I said *somewhat* deficient," whispered Tom agitatedly, "and when did they decide to bring the letters up?"

"Furthermore, we find that these girls are well cared for by their foster-mother, and are not afraid of being beaten by her."

Mrs Philpot swelled inside her corsets and a huge grin

pushed up her red cheeks so high they squeezed her eyes shut and a hairpin pinged out of her greasy topknot. Tom's palm had become very slippery. Annie laced her fingers through his.

"As regards the caning," went on the President, "in view of the direct conflict of evidence in this matter—" Annie tightened her grip on Tom's hand and pulled in a breath "—the Committee is *unable* to give a decision."

Annie let out the air in a chuckle of delighted disbelief. "Does that mean I'm not guilty?" she mouthed at Tom. In answer, he squeezed her fingers and nodded towards Fisher. His face was as long as a stirrup. Eland's was an icy mask.

"We've done it! We've won, Annie! We've WON!"

"AHEM!" The President rustled his papers meaningfully, and Tom looked suitably chastened, though he was grinning all over inside.

"After due consideration of *all* the facts," went on the President, "the Committee advises . . ." Annie's scalp twitched. A foxbrush of fear flicked across every nerve ending. ". . . that it is in the interests of elementary education in this village . . ." The President drew out a handkerchief and dabbed the back of his neck. If he had been a conjurer that handkerchief could not have commanded more rapt attention . . . "that the Head Teacher . . ." He paused to blow his nose, examine the handkerchief and replace it in his pocket ". . . should seek other employment—with as *little delay as possible.*"

There was a silence you could have nailed a picture to. Then chaos. Tom sprang to his feet, roaring, "Are you out of your mind, man? You've only proved one charge! You can't sack her for discourtesy!"

"Stop it, Tom!" Annie grabbed his elbow. "Let's keep our dignity—it's all we have left!"

"But it's *obvious*—they were going to sack you, whatever happened!"

"She brought it on herself." The sanctimonious sneer seemed to come straight from the pulpit. "It was a foregone conclusion. As I said before—an *impossible* woman!"

"You say another word about my wife, Eland, and I'll stuff your bloody head up the school chimney!"

Eland gave a gasp and sat down hard. Tom faced the President, head high. "How's that for discourtesy—Your Honour!"

He turned to take Annie's hand. But the Headmistress had gone. She had run away from school—just as she had threatened to, all those years ago. Because it wasn't her school any more.

PART 3: TERMS OF ABUSE

Come all you bold fellows that follow the plough
Either hedging or ditching or milking the cow
The time has arrived and the union flag waves
We won't be kept down like a lot of white slaves.

From Burston and Shimpling we'll meet on the Green
For the fat bellied farmers we don't care a bean
From Diss and Winfarthing and Tivetshall too
We'll come with flags flying and ribbons of blue.

You may now tell the farmers you'll be slaves no more
The starvation wages you will not endure
Though you worked night and day you could not satisfy
They treated you worse than a pig in a sty.

The farmers will very soon find I am sure
That a man is a man be he never so poor
And no better man in England can be found
Than the hardworking man who is tilling the ground.

All England will learn of our doings today
As in grand procession we all march away
And the downtrodden labourers will cry as they go
With God and Tom Higdon we'll vanquish our foe.

Union song

CHAPTER I

"So the Managers have won. And Higdons have got the boot."

George Durbidge emptied a whisky into his mouth and chewed it for a moment before swallowing. He stared a challenge round at the mournful faces in the taproom of the Crown Inn. "Didn't I tell Tom the first night he came here, there'd be trouble if he didn't kiss the print of Lady Eland's slipper?"

"You didn't know who he was then," objected the ploughboy, a married man now with his own cottage recently renovated by the Parish Council. "Called him a rabble rouser."

"And your Sabina will miss the both of them," added Harry Ellis. "She's really come on these last years."

"Oh, it's the children who'll suffer all right," said Durbidge. "And all because Eland got the wind up, in case Annie Higdon was more popular than he was! Well, you've let them walk all over you. Farmers'll make you lot jump from now on, I'll be bound!"

"That we will," rumbled Ford, bellying up to him with a full tankard slobbering foam over the cuff of his Norfolk jacket and splattering down on to his new knickerbockers. "There'll be no sloping off to Union meetings after this, eh, Fred?"

Fred looked up from his pint. He had been sitting in silence, letting the waves break over his head, his mind full of private tangles. Higdon had been good to him, got him a rise, even though he wasn't in the union. Ivy had been glad of the money, but she hadn't thanked Tom Higdon for it. "You shouldn't *need* to have other men fighting to put bread in your mouth," she told Fred. "Next thing we know we'll have the Relief Officer coming round, offering us one and six a week. You could do *anything*. I can't understand you."

94

What could he say when *he* didn't understand either? He knew that he was discovering a genuine love of the land, it made him feel real and honest. Or was he fooling himself? Was it simply that he welcomed the weariness which emptied his head at night so he could forget how he had wasted that other woman's life . . . But perhaps he was just wasting Ivy's instead?

And what about *Dora*? It was ages since they'd talked. No, that wasn't fair — she'd brought him an essay, but he'd been too tired to read it properly. He'd told her it was very good, though, wasn't that enough? When *was* that? Last year? As for Baby . . . He realized that they were waiting for him to speak and he had forgotten the question.

"Very good," he said. "Very good." He lifted his glass.

"Your wife will be pleased and all," said Ford, "her being so pally with Mrs Eland."

The glass clattered against Fred's teeth. He put it down.

"I expect so," he said.

"Well *mine* won't," said a cold quiet voice.

Ford glared round. Henry Garnham glared back, his beard quivering. If they'd had a couple of felling mallets in their hands at that moment, anything might have happened.

"Then she's a damn' fool," pronounced Ford thickly. "Even if she is my sister."

Durbidge shouldered between them to the bar.

"Give us a bottle of scotch to take home. For the missus," he explained, winking. "She mixes it with the grain for our hens, and when they fall over, she ups and wrings their necks!"

"And a stray pheasant or two, that might find its way on to your land?" asked a mocking voice. Fisher had come to gloat. Durbidge stuffed the bottle into his pocket and patted it.

"Planning to hold an Inquiry?" He gave a wide and leery grin. "Just about your style, eh? Walloping defenceless women."

"You should know. We've all seen the bruises on your wife!"

Durbidge's eyes flashed. A pulse of naked fury sent

shockwaves bouncing off the walls of the taproom. "I'll pretend I didn't hear that, Fisher," he said with the deadly calm of a viper studying a rabbit. "But I'll tell you this—if Annie Higdon wants a champion—I'm her man!"

"What are we going to *do*, Marjory?" said Violet. "The new teachers are coming next week, and Governess hasn't told us her plans yet. I'm not even sure she's got any."

They trudged on up the lane. They were supposed to be spotting March flowers for their nature notebooks, but neither of them could work up any interest.

"The trouble is," said Marjory, "she always wants to do everthing off her own bat. It puts people's backs up."

"But Burston *needs* her. People have got to help."

"What can they do? Ordinary people don't count."

They stared despondently over the fields. Everywhere, green nibs and needles were forcing their way through the black earth, promising a good harvest later in the year. Soon Governess and Master would be gone, and the people of Burston would carry on ploughing and sowing and reaping as if they had no more choice in the matter than the corn had about whether it should grow or not . . . Violet caught Marjory's arm and stopped dead.

"Remember what Governess said about how Unity is Strength?"

Marjory nodded sadly.

"Well, that's what keeps Burston together, isn't it? All our fathers working the land for the farmers. But what if . . . what if they all *stopped* working?"

"You mean—if they went on *strike*?" Marjory was horrified. "They wouldn't dare."

"Well, what did Mr Higdon start the unions for, then?" cried Violet despairingly. "I thought they were so we could help each other."

"But this is school business, not farming business."

"It *is* farming business. The farmers wanted them sacked just as much as Eland did. And they're all School Managers."

"Well, then, they've won. The unions will probably pack up once Mr Higdon's gone. Anyway, if there was a strike, he'd get the blame, and they'd only send in the troops to do the work."

Violet walked over to a nearby oak tree and punched it hard. She took all the skin off her knuckles and didn't feel a thing.

"So nobody's going to do anything? Well, *I* am!"

"What can *you* do? Nobody listens to children."

"Oh, no?" A new idea was growing behind Violet's eyes, filling up her face with light. "Then we'll MAKE them listen! If the grown-ups won't go on strike — WE will!"

"Well," said Annie Higdon, tipping up the watch pinned to the front of her frilled bosom and looking at it, "I think that's enough for today. Who wants to ring the bell?" She looked round at the circle of tilted faces. "Hetty? You're usually keen."

Hetty went a petunia pink and drooped her head over the offending hands, squeezing them punishingly together.

"Please, Madam?" called Emily in a shaky voice. "Nobody wants to ring it. Because it'll mean it's the end of the day. And . . . and nobody wants it to end."

Annie told her husband afterwards that it was worth a lifetime's teaching to hear one child say those words. She turned away for a moment, her face grasping unshed tears. Then, "Oh, my dears," she said, moving to embrace them all, "my last afternoon is nearly over . . . "

There was a scrimmage of hugs. Everyone was crying and holding on to someone else. Grieving, they rocked together like a single person. Mrs Higdon gently disengaged herself and, pulling out a hanky nearly as big as a bedsheet, gave her nose a force nine blow.

"Now, then!" She opened her desk drawer and rustled inside. "There's an orange and an Easter egg here for everybody!"

The bell rang rather late. Mrs Higdon rang it herself. After the last of many leave-takings, husband and wife collected their things and walked out arm in arm like a pair of lovers into the spring afternoon.

On the pretence that they were going to take down the wall displays, Violet kept everyone behind, except Sam Todd and one or two others she didn't think she could trust. Everyone knew something was afoot, but nobody had suspected such a daring plan.

"We can't strike!" protested Mabel. "We'll get whacked!"

"Who'll whack us? We haven't got any teachers! We'll refuse to be taught by the new ones, and we'll stay out until Mr and Mrs Higdon get their jobs back! They won't send troops against *us*, and they can't blame Governess and Master if we don't tell them what we're going to do!"

"But what about our parents? Won't they get into trouble?"

"Why should they? It's our decision. We owe it to Governess to show the Education people how much we love her. And it won't last more than a day. Oh, *please*," begged Violet. "Say you'll join me — or I'll do it alone."

She'd got them now, and she knew it. "Right, then! I've made a list of all your names. If you're with me, I'll put a tick — and don't *shove*!"

She ticked off the names so fast her hand seemed to blur. Then she came to Dora.

"I don't know. Can I tell you tomorrow?"

Violet chewed the inside of her cheek and looked at her, tapping the pencil against her thumbnail.

"I know what you think," said Dora. "Mrs Higdon's been good to me . . . "

"Never mind." Violet cut her off briskly. "So long as your Auntie Ivy don't warn Eland. Remember, everybody, don't tell your parents unless you can trust them! And don't tell Governess!"

She picked a piece of chalk out of the box on the desk and reached up to the board.

"This'll give the new teachers something to choke on!" she giggled, and in her best handwriting she inscribed the words:

WE ARE GOING ON STRIKE!

They turned the board to face the wall, rushed out into the porch and chalked the words up again. "Let's put messages up all over the village! Outside the Rectory as well!" shouted Emily.

"Better do it after they've gone to bed," warned Marjory.

"All right. Let's go and see what's happening on the Green!"

To their amazement, the Burston grown-ups had also overcome any fears that speaking up for the Higdons might bring trouble, and were holding their own protest by the light of two huge flares borrowed from George Durbidge's cockle stall. Tom and Annie watched from a distance. "Any decisions they make must be their own," said Tom. "But if we've given them the strength to fight back, so much the better."

The turnout was astonishing. Farm workers, railwaymen, domestic servants and housewives jostled to make their voices heard.

"Remember the time Governess took our lad to live with them when we had whooping cough at home?" shouted one mother.

"Tom Higdon put his hand in his own pocket to pay for schoolbooks!" called another. The tributes went on and on. Even Jimmy Wittle's mum yelled out "NEW TROUSERS!" then shrank back blushing into the crowd. Durbidge elected himself chairman.

"Quiet, everyone! This is the plan. We're going to write to the Education Committee and complain that their Inquiry was rigged. Make 'em send the new supply teachers packing. And the Barnardo brats—they're not fit to get schooled with decent folks' children. I'll draft out the letter, put it in pretty words, and if they refuse to listen to us, well, dammit, we pay our rates and I reckon we've got some rights! So three cheers for the Higdons, and the Rector can stuff his opinions right up his—"

He was drowned out by roars of approval.

"Stick like shit to a blanket!" roared Durbidge by way of

concluding his oration and the whole company took up the cry.

Behind the net curtains of the Rectory, Mrs Eland was cowering in horrified fascination, while the Reverend paced the carpet, green in the face with fury.

"Come away from there, for goodness' sake," he snarled. "It's all moonshine, they'll have forgotten about it by tomorrow."

"What are you going to do, dear?" asked his wife, casting an anxious eye over her china as the Reverend swept past a small table loaded with fancy porcelain, the tails of his coat wagging with wrath. "I mean, if they *don't* forget about it?"

He swung round, and a Staffordshire shepherdess sailed on to the carpet and smashed into shivers. He looked at it.

"*Then I'll break them!*" he said.

CHAPTER 2

"Rhubarb jam, dear? Or would you prefer gooseberry?"

Breakfast time in the schoolhouse, 1 April 1914. A morning much the same as any other. Tom Higdon had his nose in a book, a pencil between his teeth and a half-written speech on his knee. His wife had butter in her hair, a slice of charred bread in each hand and a harrassed look on her face. Tom considered her question. "Erm . . . rhubarb, please, dear."

"*Rhubarb?* Oh . . . that's a pity."

"What is?" A tinge of irritation crept into Tom's voice. He fought it down. "What's a pity?" he repeated less testily.

"Oh, nothing, dear . . . If I scrape off the mould, I'm sure it'll be perfectly eatable . . . Oh! Was that someone at the door?"

"Five minutes past seven," said Tom. "They haven't wasted any time." He got up.

"Stay there and finish your breakfast," she commanded, forgetting that he hadn't had any yet. "I'll deal with this."

She opened the door.

"Good morning! It's Mr Ikin, dear!" she called over her shoulder. "Assistant General to the Education Committee, no less! To what do we owe the honour?"

Ikin paled a little at his boisterous welcome. He took a step back, steadying his top hat while extending his other hand. Between the index and middle fingers were two envelopes.

"Your pay cheques," he said flatly. "In lieu of notice."

"How very thoughtful!" beamed the Headmistress. "And what exactly does *in lieu of notice* mean?"

"We respectfully request that you vacate the schoolhouse at your earliest convenience. The new teachers have arrived, and—"

"They have my sympathy," was the smiling rejoinder.

"And you may tell the Committee that it will be convenient for us to depart when our three months' notice is up and not one second before. So I suggest you take yourself and your blood money back where you came from, because *we're* staying put!"

"I'd advise you to reconsider," yelped Ikin, flinging the envelopes on to the hall table and dancing back a couple of feet as Tom loomed up at him, fists clenched. "And if you're not out of here by the end of the week . . ." His yelps diminished to a series of defiant yaps ". . . steps will be taken to have you removed — by force if necessary!"

"*Good morning*, Mr Ikin!"

The door slammed.

As Ikin hastened across the playground, he noticed one or two children on the scrubby patch of common in front of the Crown Inn, playing a game with a lot of little red flags. It was only when he entered the school porch and saw what Violet had written there, that he realized just what kind of game it was. He spurted round to the Rectory, and the Reverend's telephone wire was soon twanging a distress call to the Diss Constabulary.

By now everybody except the Higdons knew what was up. Porridge plates on kitchen tables had been pushed aside and replaced by bowls of paste, crayons and paints and card (borrowed from the classroom) for the making of posters and placards.

"It's just like being back at school!" chuckled Mrs Boulton, the postmistress, as she put the finishing touches to a gigantic banner proclaiming: **JUSTICE!** in letters two feet high.

Not everyone was in such good spirits, however. On the other side of the village, Mrs Philpot was nailing a poster of her own to a tree in her front garden. It too bore a single word: **VICTORY!** "And if anyone tries to pull it down," she growled, "I'll tear the face off them!"

No preparations of any kind were in hand inside Blossom Cottage.

"I absolutely forbid you to get involved in this hare-brained scheme!" Ivy told Dora. "The idea!"

"But it isn't fair! On Mr and Mrs Higdon, I mean..."

"You know very well what I think of those two. They overstepped the mark and now they've got to face the music."

"They shouldn't have sacked them — should they, Dad?"

"No," he said slowly. "I don't reckon they should."

"Oh, you don't care," Ivy scissored straight through him. "So long as you can get drunk every night in the Crown with a notorious Bolshevik — "

"Tom's a Socialist, and he never has more than one glass..."

"But of course, if you want to ruin your children's education and probably their whole lives..."

Snip, snip, shredding him into little pieces until he could only mutter lamely, "Well, it's just a protest. Won't last more than a day."

"It'll be on their records. What chance will Dora have then of getting a decent job?"

"But the new teachers might not like me," said Dora. "Mrs Higdon said I was special..."

"If you're special, the new teachers will find it out. If not, you'll have to accept that Mrs Higdon was stringing you along for reasons of her own. Off you go now, girls. And remember, people who strike, people who don't conform, never get a second chance."

Shamefaced, Dora set out with Alex for the Council School. If this strike works, she thought, it'll make history. In years to come, people will be reading books about Violet and Marjory — But they won't be reading about me...

Five other children were huddled at the gates, guarded by Mrs Ling, Fisher, the Chief Constable of Diss and two young policemen. Ikin emerged from the school visibly shaken, having just taken the new master and mistress for a tour round the premises. On entering the classroom, he had spotted the blackboard facing the wall and turned it round with a flourish. A second later, he was wishing he could give Violet Potter a few strikes of his own.

Inside the Rectory, Mrs Eland was pretending to hem a cushion cover, while keeping a watchful eye on her husband who was pretending to read a book of eighteenth century sermons. Tension settled like dust on the porcelain. She felt as if she were waiting for a monstrous sneeze to blow her drawing room to smithereens...

"Right!" shouted Violet. "Is everybody ready?"

There was a roar of enthusiasm as mothers and children raised their banners and surged forward.

"BACK!" Violet held up a hand — Just like Mrs Higdon on the first day. They backed. "Shush a minute! *Listen*!" The familiar clang, clang of the bell sounded a challenge from the school. Violet straightened her shoulders and bellowed, "Banners aloft!"

As if in answer, an April gust filled up Mrs Boulton's pennant, nearly lifting the children on either side clean off the ground. It bulged out, as proud and taut and magnificent as Farmer Ford's great belly. Violet filled up her lungs.

"Forward — March!"

"Did you hear something, Tom?"

Mrs Higdon raised the curtain and looked out. She rubbed her eyes and looked again . . . And let out a whoop of laughter.

"It's no laughing matter," complained her husband.

"Oh, but it *is*, Tom! Come and see!"

"Come and see what? Has the Rector arrived with a barrow to take away our furniture?"

"If you'd close your mouth for one minute, Tom, and open up your ears, you might hear something to gladden your heart."

"What d'you mean?"

"Hush, Tom and *listen* !"

And then, very softly at first, but growing louder and louder, he heard:

"We want our teachers back! We want our teachers back! Justice! Justice! We want our teachers back!"

"What on earth . . . ?"

"It's the children! The wonderful, marvellous children! Violet's called them out on strike! The school's gone *on strike*!"

Tom tore open the door and they gazed out at an armada of banners, soaring and swooping above the marching children and their mothers. In nearby fields, others were gazing too. Men waved their hoes and pruning hooks, and lifted their voices to cheer.

"We can't call her Violet any more!" said Tom. "It's the wrong colour! We'll have to call her RED! Red Potter, the worker's friend! Give us a chorus of the Red Flag, Violet!"

Violet grinned, saluted and started bawling out the workers' anthem. They marched on, right past the school gates where Ikin and the others stood, tranced with rage, like unwilling spirits summoned up from their tombs to waver ineffectually in the sunlight. Dora hung her head and stepped inside.

"Round the Candlestick!" ordered Violet, and they set off on a circular route, taking in most of the village. As they strutted past Mrs Philpot's cottage, the good woman herself erupted from her door, brandishing a dustpan and brush with the intention of swiping off a few heads and gathering them up afterwards.

"I'll tin the lot of you!" she screamed.

"Tin yourself!" retorted Mrs Potter, swinging round with her small fists up in front of her. Routed, Mrs Philpot dived back indoors, and Mrs Potter fell back into step, bombinating, "We'll keep the Red Flag flying here!"

On they went, past the Old Mill, over the Village Green and up to the Rectory, where Violet called for "Three Boos for the Parson!" They finished up back in front of the Crown Inn, and Mrs Boulton handed out mixed nuts and peppermint lumps, and dispensed lemonade from a bucket.

After a quick swig, Violet climbed up on to a crate.

"We all know why we're here!" she shouted. "To fight for all the things Governess and Master have been teaching us these last years. Brotherhood! Freedom! Equality! And Justice! What the managers did to Mr and Mrs Higdon was INjustice, and until it's put right, we're not going to go back to school! (There were cheers at this.) I want to thank everybody for giving us sweets and things and showing your support the way you have. Sixty-six out of seventy-two children have come out on strike. Burston's a proud village today. As for the blacklegs — well, some of them can't be blamed I suppose — but I hope they always remember that they didn't do as they were done to. Mr and Mrs Higdon are our friends, and we're going to get them their jobs back, and have the kind of schooling *we* want — the kind that'll give us a better future and help us be bigger people. Bread and Roses!"

"BREAD AND ROSES!"

The tidal wave of approval nearly knocked her off the crate. This is how Mr Higdon felt, she thought dizzily. This is what it feels like when you know you're right. When you want people to have the great and beautiful things in life as well as the ordinary simple ones. And when they want it too. The thought was so awesome, she got down and went for a second glass of lemonade.

While this was going on, Eland made as dignified a way to the schoolhouse as he might, with the Sexton treading on his shadow and unctuously assuring him, "It'll be a nine days' wonder, dear sir. They are all April Fools!"

Eland swatted him aside, and raised a thunderbolt-bearing fist to smite the door. It opened before the blow could connect and he tumbled forward, grabbing the lintel just in time to save his face from plunging into Annie Higdon's matronly bosom.

"Yes?" she said, her face pulled very straight, though something was tweaking impertinently at the corners of her lips.

Mr Eland steadied himself, fizzing with rage. He reminded Annie of a thin black bottle full of nasty medicine which somebody had shaken too hard. She half expected his hat to blow off at any second. He flung a long black spurt of arm out behind him in the direction of Crown Common, the white fingers shuddering like froth on the end of it.

"*Your* doing, I take it?"

"Not guilty, Your Honour. They did it all by themselves."

"But you knew about it! That's just as bad."

"None of my pupils breathed a word," was the cheerful reply. "Tom was absolutely staggered, weren't you, dear?"

The Rector's face was a fistful of white knuckles clutching back screams of frustration. Beads of sweat came out on it like boils. He pushed his lips together and breathed through his nose until the urge to jump up and down on his hat and rip out handfuls of hair — his own, and anybody else's within reach — had abated sufficiently to allow normal speech. He bared his teeth and spoke through them.

"He who sows the wind shall reap the whirlwind!" he frothed at the radiant Headmistress.

"Then I'd hold on to my hat if I were you," she replied chirpily.

"Have a care, Mrs Higdon, have a care!" snarled Eland, his lips speckled with flecks of saliva. "Remember Isaiah! *I shall dash them in pieces like a potter's vessel!*"

"Quite. But the Potters in this case are made of sterner stuff. And they're all on *our* side. Along with most of the village. Good morning!"

The gust from the front door slamming blew Eland almost into the arms of his Sexton who murmured solicitously, "A nine days' wonder, sir, that's all it'll be, you mark my—" and got a shove in the chest for his pains as Eland lurched past, rabid with wrath.

"I will smite them hip and thigh!" he slavered, as he staggered back to the Rectory. "Yes — that's *it!*"

He stopped dead, and the Sexton walked into him, biting his tongue.

"Hit them where it hurts!" said Eland triumphantly, eyes glinting. "In their pockets! Once these idlers and hangers-on start to feel the pinch, they'll drop off those ranting braggarts like fleas from a dead dog!"

"Corinthians?" mumbled the Sexton, frowning as he tried to place the quotation and feeling a blister come up on his tongue.

"No, my dear fellow — Eland. Chapter and verse!"

CHAPTER 3

"Take an hour for dinner," said Violet. "We march again at one!"

And march they did. All through that afternoon and the morning and the afternoon of the day after and the day after that. For if parents and children were determined to get their teachers back, their enemies were equally determined that they should not.

"Then we won't go to church either!" declared Mrs Wilby, Emily's mother. "We'll have our own services on the Green."

"Good idea," mused Tom. "We could invite a few Union men to come and speak too — I know the railwaymen are with us . . . "

"And every morning before we march," went on Mrs Wilby, "we want you to take prayers, Annie, just like you used to."

Mrs Higdon was delighted. After prayers, the protesters set off every day with their banners and paper trimmings, to which were cheekily added all the threatening notes from the attendance officer.

The notes were soon followed by summonses to the parents to appear in court. The Education Committee were bringing charges.

"What did I tell you?" said Ivy. "Aren't you glad you kept out of it now, Dora?" Dora said nothing. Just carried on praying she could catch chickenpox or whooping cough or anything rather than creep out early every day with Baby and run home early to avoid Violet and the marchers.

On the day of the hearing, parents and children set off in procession from the crossways at nine-thirty sharp. To their astonishment, the streets of Diss were lined with well-wishers who had been awaiting their arrival since early in the morning.

Mabel Plumtree happily posed for the photographers, shaking her madeira coloured curls (tortured in rags all the night before). Then the parents went into court, while the young strikers raced to the park where Mrs Wilby bought them some ginger beer.

The Magistrates looked askance at the large number of defendants, none of whom denied absenting their children from school, though all pleaded not guilty to breaking the law.

"We didn't send them because it was unfair to turn our teachers away," Mrs Potter told the Chairman. "And we won't send them unless there's a Public Inquiry. I don't see why we should be ruled by the Parson!"

"I cannot order an Inquiry," replied the Chairman. "I can only deal with this case. Fined two shillings and sixpence. Next case! Mr George Durbidge—Did you absent your daughter Sabina from the Council Sch—"

"Before you start your interrogation," said Durbidge, "I've something to say." He gripped the rail of the dock. "It's not us who are on trial here. It's The Powers That Be. We know why the Education Committee don't want a Public Inquiry—they're afraid the truth might come out. Well, the truth is what we want. We're all satisfied with the education our children have received, and we believe the teachers have been done an injustice. Prove us wrong and we'll send the children back. Until then, we take our own course."

"Thank you for your edifying comments, Mr Durbidge," said the President drily. "Defendant is fined two and six, and reminded that it is not appropriate for individuals or individual parishes to take the law into their own hands. Mr Harry Ling!" The bootmender stood up. "Did you wilfully absent your daughter Marjory from school on April the first of this year?"

"Well, sir, she went off at the usual time. And when she got there, she joined the strikers. What was I to do? Was I to force her into school against her will?" There was general laughter.

The Chairman drew his robes about him haughtily. "What would you do if she did anything else you did not want her to?"

Mrs Ling stood up. "We've a conscientious objection to her going to school."

"Really? And what is that?"

"She'd sit all alone and fret and pine for the Teacher."

The Chairman's eyebrows collided and the eyes beneath them fastened suspiciously on the woman. But she wasn't joking. He looked round at the other parents. In their faces he read nothing but passionate concern.

"Hrrrmm! The court is aware of the affection felt by the people of Burston for the Mistress and Master. Be that as it may, we are bound to uphold the prosecution brought by the Education Committee. All Defendants are fined half a crown and warned that further behaviour of this sort will be dealt with very differently."

The parents emerged to loud hoorays from the crowd and waiting children. Tom strode up and shook every one of them by the hand. Then a man arrived with one of the new movie cameras, and took their photos for the "living pictures". The film was shown later in the Corn Hall.

The procession re-formed and set off for the market place, where Durbidge passed round the hat and collected enough money for them all to have bread and cheese.

"We'll have to get organized," he announced. "Have a proper Strike Committee — I'll be Chairman — to get cash for the fines, because you can bet your boots we'll be back in court a fair few times before we're done."

"Know what I think?" said Annie. "I'm already taking prayers — why don't I carry on and teach the whole day as well?"

"Where?"

"On the Village Green." She giggled. "Right in front of the church! It's glorious weather, and I don't want my children getting behind because of this strike. Boycotting the Council School is all very well, but we need to offer an alternative."

"The woman's a genius!" exclaimed Durbidge. "They

won't be able to touch us if we're sending our children to the school of our choice. It's our right!"

Next morning, Mrs Higdon arrived with a new register and drew up timetables for the day. There were a few muted grumbles from one or two pupils who had been hoping to spend the rest of their schooldays marching round Burston, but everyone agreed it was the best way to beat the Committee. Lessons were conducted on the Green to the fascination of reporters and the increasing anger of the Rector, who took to entering and leaving his church with his eyes fixed straight ahead and his teeth clenched. The parents were summonsed again and the fine increased to five shillings, which Durbidge collected in the streets of Diss.

Tom and Annie moved into the Old Mill and looked about for somewhere they could teach on rainy days. Then they had a real bit of luck. Old Ambrose, the blind man, offered them a room above his disused carpenter's shop — on the far side of the Green but still directly visible from the church gate. It wasn't much of a place, but, after a coat of whitewash, better than Eton in Mrs Higdon's opinion. They entered by means of a ladder propped against the wall.

Meanwhile, Durbidge used every scrap of publicity he could to get donations from all over the country for books and furniture, including a whole guinea from an anonymous donor in Brighton. After this, there were no more summonses because nobody could deny that the children were receiving a satisfactory education.

Every Sunday, in between services, there were meetings. Parents and teachers from neighbouring schools came to show their support, sometimes five hundred at a time, and union leaders too, even the President of the Trades Council in Lowestoft. From a ragged little hamlet no one had ever heard of, Burston had blossomed into a centre for revolutionary debate. Men and women who had been brought up to doff the cap or curtsey to their "betters", now held their heads high and talked about how they could make the world better for everyone.

One day when Violet was passing the Rectory, the Reverend sprang out into her path like a black bedspring.

"Don't run away!" he commanded. Violet had no intention of doing any such thing. "Just tell me," said Eland, glancing cautiously about, "what is this — this *power* that Mrs Higdon has over you all?"

"It's simple," said Violet. "She cares about us."

"And I don't?" He looked like a candle somebody had just blown out. "A man chosen by God to care for you?"

Violet felt almost sorry for him. She tried to explain. "You know Jimmy Wittle's dad? How he gets drunk every night and shouts about England being great and punches people and then sicks up over everybody?"

The Rector's eyes slitted. "I fail to — "

"Well, Mrs Higdon says he does it because he knows secretly that he *isn't* great and it makes him angry and the only way he can pretend to be great is by hitting people."

"I see." Eland's lips curled with disdain. "You're saying that Mrs Higdon's brand of education will turn all Burston's hooligans into Prime Ministers?"

"No — But knowledge is strength, Governess says. Like unity. The more that people find out about the world, the more they'll care about it, and if they've got something to care about, maybe they won't hate themselves so much."

"What utter taradiddle!" The Rector struck his forehead. "I suppose you've never heard the saying, A little knowledge is a Dangerous Thing?"

"Only to folk who want to keep all the knowledge for themselves," Violet replied. "And why should they want to do that, Reverend? Why should they want us to stay ignorant?"

"You little horror!" The spiteful yellow face bubbled like toasted cheese. "Clear off before I teach you a lesson you *won't* like!"

"Well done!" said the Headmistress when Violet told her of the encounter. "And you know what makes me really proud? It's that people will always remember that the Burston School Strike was started by a woman — for that's practically what you are — to fight for another woman who'd been done down. By the way, did you know that the colours of the Suffragettes' flag represent the words: Give Votes to Women! — and that they are Green, White and *Violet!*"

Current affairs was now a favourite lesson — especially since the papers often contained news about the pupils themselves. One day Emily brought in a small item, for want of anything better, and read it out to the class.

"It says that in Saraj — Saraj — I can't say this word . . ."

"Sarajevo," prompted Mrs Higdon, pronouncing it Sarayayvoh, and squinting over Emily's shoulder at the creased square of newsprint. "It says that Archduke Ferdinand has been shot there. Assassinated! What d'you think of that, children?"

"If it ain't Burston," yelled Billy, "it don't count!"

Mrs Higdon looked at him over the top of her glasses.

"Billy! After all that's been done for you by people all over England who've never even seen you, so that you can finish your education and grow up into a caring citizen. I'm ashamed." She gazed round at the class. "Archduke Ferdinand was heir to the Austrian throne. And what touches Austria, touches Burston."

That was June. By July, folks began to see what she meant.

CHAPTER 4

"There's going to be a war," said Marjory Ling.
"Who with?" asked Mabel.
"Kaiser Bill. Boss of Germany."

A conversation at playtime, just before school was due to close for the summer. In the Crown Inn that evening, the menfolk were swapping much the same comments.

"What's it all about, then?"
"Search me."
"Well I'm going to fight. You get good wages in the army."
"You'll none of you be rushing off before the harvest's in, I hope." This from Fisher.
"The women'll manage. Anyway, it'll be over by Christmas."
"Says who? Tom Higdon? You won't catch him enlisting!"
"He's too old. But he'll be recruiting, you can bet."
"If his wife lets him! Well maybe those striking brats will come to their senses now. Learn what's important."
"They're fighting for what's right. Same as what we'll be."
"I thought you didn't know why you were fighting."
"For England. And because the King says so. And to get away from the likes of you."

Meanwhile, Eland was drawing up battle plans of his own. One hot afternoon, Blind Ambrose hailed Violet as she was about to ascend the ladder to a meeting in the carpenter's shop.

"I'd know your footsteps anywhere!" he chortled. "No nonsense Potter! I've had a letter, Vi. Can you read it for me?"

Violet opened the official-looking communication. Her face scrunched with disbelief.

"They're going to put you off your land!" she gasped. "The Rector's taking back your Glebe!"

Glebe land was leased by the church to smallholders. For many it was their main source of income. When times got bad they could sell their produce and live on potatoes and bread. When they were good, there were always salads and fruit on the table.

"You know why he's done this, don't you?" said Violet. "To pay you out for letting us have the shop as a school. And I bet you're not the only one!"

Violet was right. Henry Garnham got a similar letter that day, and so did Harry Ling the bootmender.

"He said he'd get back at you if I wouldn't go to court and tell a lie!" sobbed Marjory.

"Never mind," soothed her father. "We're in the right and nobody can take *that* away. But poor old Garnham! It's because he goes to Strike meetings I suppose. And to think his boy's gone away to fight for his country!"

News got round quickly. Fred Watson was horrified.

"Can you believe he'd stoop so low, Ivy? A man of God!"

"He's within his rights and probably has very good reasons," replied his wife with apparent composure, though she was inwardly rattled by this latest turn of events.

"And we all know what *they* are," said Dora. "The Inspectors said the Strike School was perfectly fit for the children, so now he's trying blackmail to get people back to the old one."

"That's a wicked thing to say!"

"And a wickeder to do!"

"A *blind* man, Ivy," said Dad. "How can you justify that?"

"I shall ask Charles myself, after church."

"Well I'm not going," said Dora. "And neither is Alex."

"Her name is Alexandra! And you're both old enough to obey your own consciences, I'm sure. But you're not to go to Strike services. You can read the Bible at home. What about you, Fred? Will you come with me?"

"I'd better supervise the girls' reading."

For once, Ivy had no answer.

To make matters worse, Eland offered Harry Ling's plot of land to the Sexton — *William* Ling, Harry's *brother*. It was only a bit of an acre at the back of their house, but to everyone's astonishment, William accepted. He came round without a word of notice and started cutting all Harry's plum trees level with the hedge.

"Judas!" screamed Marjory out of the window. "To think my mum came and nursed your whole family through scarlet fever when everybody told her she could catch it herself! You ought to be ashamed of yourself, you horrible old man!"

"Please," begged her mother, trying to drag Marjory back in by her skirt. "Don't make a scene. Your father's not well."

"And whose fault is that?"

"God will provide. He always has."

Marjory pulled away from her in a fury, and yelled out over the mutilated bushes: "Well, isn't it time somebody told the Rector that he *isn't* God? Because it looks to me as if he's providing all right — providing *some people* get on their knees and bow down to him!"

"I'm BOILED!" said Alex for the fiftieth time.

Last afternoon of the Harvest holidays. Hot metal sky shimmering over toasted crops. Not a cloud. Not a puff of wind to ruffle the nap of the shaven cornfields where women and children, bums upwards and chins almost touching their knees, shuffled to glean up the husks left behind by the toppling blades.

The resting horses stood about in the heat, motionless and heavy as old furniture. In the nearby shade, their drivers swilled the desert out of their throats with glitteringly cold cider from deep stone bottles. Cows, fiercely black and white in the hammering light, flicked and munched in a dream of flies. The still air prickled like pepper.

Sprawled in the scratchy grass at the top of a slight incline, Dora and Alex watched the workers. Van Gogh had his nose in a muslin bag which had been round the picnic cheese, and was trying to pull it off with a weary paw. He whined disconsolately, and Dora reached over to free him, then rolled on to her back, letting the heat press down and flatten her. She closed her eyes.

"I'm going home," grumbled Alex. "There's nothing to do and no one to talk to and I'm boiling to death, and you don't care."

"Suit yourself," said Dora. She heard her sister's feet kicking through the dry turf, and the beat of VG's paws as he jumped up eagerly.

"Shove off, dog," said Alex. The footsteps faded. Dora felt VG's nose, dry and rough as an unsoaked prune, pushing itself into her ear. She flung an arm out and pulled him close. Alex was right. Nobody to play with, nobody to talk to. Outcasts. Blacklegs. Not that Violet or Marjory were openly hostile. They just weren't interested — too many meetings to organize, letters to write. Their parents' attitude was rather different, especially after the Glebe business. Dad didn't drink in the Crown any more.

Why can't we just be like the others, Dora asked herself? I won't ever get anywhere now, the new teachers think I'm stupid.

As a matter of fact, Dora had got very lazy recently. It didn't seem right to work for people who had taken away the Higdons' livelihood. Not that they were starving — the villagers saw to that. But there was another reason for not working — the lurking suspicion that maybe Governess really *had* been stringing her along, as Ivy had suggested. That she wasn't special at all, it was just something people said, like Dad, to keep you happy.

She felt something tickly dropping on to her nose and a shadow turned the red glare behind her eyelids black. She opened her eyes, squinting. Sam Todd, the farmer's son, was standing over her, blowing dandelion seeds down on to her face. She sat up.

"Hey. Stop that." Little pest! It was bad enough having to sit next to the big lump in school without him tagging around during the holidays. He grinned at her.

"I got a penny," he said importantly.

"Lucky old you."

"For keeping a secret. Give us another penny and I'll tell you what it is."

"You can keep your old secrets . . ." She gave a sharp cry of alarm as VG jumped up at Sam, tail wagging, tongue out ready to lick the smile off him. "Van Gogh — NO !" Sam leapt back, pudgy arms beating wildly, his fat cheeks squidging with fear.

"Gerrimoff! Gerrimoff!"

Dora grabbed VG and sat him down. "Don't be such a booby, Sam. He only wants to play."

"What's going on here?" It was Sam's father, ambling up, jovial and beefy with a face as full of craters as a crumpet and buttered with sweat. "Has the little brat been plaguing you?" He gave Sam a clip round the ear. "Stop blubbering, you dolt . . . By Gor!" The farmer stared at VG and laughed. "That's a queer beast! Where d'you get that?"

"He was a Christmas present," said Dora frigidly. "From my father."

"Oh, Fred Watson? A good man, give him my regards."

You wouldn't say that if he'd done what's right and stuck by the Higdons, thought Dora. She picked up Van Gogh. "I will. Thank you, Mr Todd."

As she walked away, she heard Sam whinging, "He ain't a good man!" followed by the sound of another ear getting clouted and loud wails of protest about a penny and a secret. A silence followed, then a low whispering, and a sudden blurt of laughter from the farmer.

"That'll teach him to side with the lame dogs!"

"Lame dogs indeed!" said Dora indignantly. She tickled VG's chin expertly and he writhed with delight. She looked at him. "But you're definitely a *dirty* dog! What *have* you been doing?"

CHAPTER 5

As soon as he spotted Dora unhooking the tin bath from the kitchen wall, Van Gogh's knob of tail dropped. She picked him up and he went rigid, pushing his paws into her chest and straining away from her, good eye and jaw clenched shut in desperation. Then she lowered him into the suds and he stood, ear flattened, while she applied the tortures of carbolic and hot water.

When the water was black and Van Gogh back to his usual gingery red, she lifted him out and swathed him in a huge towel. He shrugged if off, shook himself, and became a vibrating skeleton in a whirling, dog-shaped cloud of flying droplets. Then Dora needed the towel more than he did.

An hour later, when both were dry again and comfortably full of dinner, all was forgiven. Dog and mistress were soon fast asleep.

A door slammed in her heart and Dora jolted awake. Then realized it was someone banging the knocker downstairs. She sat up in the darkness. Heard the bolt squeak below and a voice she recognized but couldn't place. She felt for the tinder box and lit a candle. Sullen, angry blooms of sound were coming up, but no distinct words. Dad's voice now, gentler, pleading. Then the door slammed again and the house was quiet. She glanced across at Alex, asleep on her back and snoring delicately with little puffing grunts. Very quietly, she swung her legs out of bed and tiptoed from the room, closing the door gingerly behind her.

Ivy was in her usual chair, knitting savagely, lips clamped in a thin line. Dad was putting on his outdoor jacket. When he saw Dora, he stopped with one arm in and one out.

"What are you doing out of bed?"

"I heard something. Is everything all right?" There was a hiss from Ivy like water dropping on cinders. The needles clacked. Dad pushed his other arm through the empty sleeve and shrugged the jacket round him.

"Everything's fine. Back to bed."

"But where are you—"

"No arguments. Bed. This minute."

She turned reluctantly. Put her foot on the first step and looked back, hearing a funny tinkling sound. Dad was stuffing something into his pocket.

"What now?" His features were thick with irritation.

"Nothing," she faltered, quenched. "Good-night, that's all."

"Good-night, love." His voice was gentle again, but there was a tenseness in him which seemed to start with whatever he was gripping inside his pocket, gripping so hard that the effort ran all the way up his arm and filled his body. He looked like something sealed shut with frost that might snap in half at a sudden movement. He was waiting for her to leave. Ivy's needles clicked faster. She was waiting too. Dora crept back upstairs. Sleep returned briefly, then something woke her up again.

"Van Gogh?" she muttered drowsily. "Is that you?" She had thought she heard his bark—Not the Hello, How are you? Is it time to play? bark, but a plaintive protesting one, a straining at the lead to get away from whoever's at the other end of it kind of bark. He sounded frightened, in pain.

Dora pulled the bedclothes off her face and listened hard. Nothing. Probably a dream. She closed her eyes.

There it was again. Only more distant. A thin spiralling howl. Then silence. She got up. In the darkness, she felt her way along the corridor, past the tight shut and uninviting door of *their* room, and down the stairs. In the kitchen she lit the oil lamp and went over to the back door. The bolt slipped aside silently. Raising the lamp, she winced barefoot across the yard, knelt down and peered inside the kennel.

It was empty.

Fear rushed up in her as flame rushes up an oil-steeped wick. She blundered back into the kitchen, looking round wildly. Then a memory rattled inside her head. A tinkling sound . . . Dad's hand thrust into his pocket. She knew now what it was. She went over to the mantelpiece where they kept VG's lead . . . It wasn't there.

"What on earth are you doing?"

Dora's heart gave a bang like a paper bag bursting. "IVY!"

"It's five o'clock. What are you doing, creeping about?"

"Where's Van Gogh?" cried Dora. "What's happened to him?"

In the lamplight, Ivy's face was a skull, fear stretched over it tauter than skin. "Van Gogh?" she whispered.

"He's not outside," Dora almost shrieked. "Something's happened to him, something terrible — "

"Nonsense!" Ivy snatched up the lamp and carried it over to the table. "Fred's taken him to work with him, that's all, he had an early start." She fiddled with the knob. The flame flowered and light widened the room. Ivy's shadow blazed up on the wall behind her, then shrank as she stepped back. Her face was normal again.

"Now, since we're all wide awake, how about a cup of tea?"

It was impossible to concentrate in class. As the day wore on, Dora grew more and more convinced that something was wrong. At dinner-time Ivy cycled over to the school with a message.

"Auntie Win's expecting you for tea, had you forgotten? You're to stay over."

Forgotten? She didn't remember ever having been told. Ivy propped the bike against the school wall and walked back home. She was sweating, Dora noticed. Of course, it was killingly hot. Or was there another reason? Maybe she'd *already* hot-pedalled it to Diss and back to "remind" Auntie Win of the invitation? Her suspicions solidified into a huge clot of fear clogging up the inside of her chest.

When the bell went, she loaded Alex into the basket on the front and set off, standing on the pedals to get leverage. Her calf muscles were twanging like harps by the time she arrived.

"Can't stop," she told the old lady, "Ivy needs me. Can you bring Alex to school tomorrow in the trap?"

She hurtled home, flung the bike against the apple tree in the front garden and raced through the parlour into the kitchen. Ivy had her back to her and was ironing tea towels. She gave a start at Dora's sudden entrance, then a sigh. She might have been expecting her.

"Where's Van Gogh?"

Ivy flipped over the tea towel, smoothed it and added it to the pile. Picked up another.

"Van Gogh?" Her voice sounded so natural it was unnatural. "Why, he'll be in when your father gets home."

"Will he?" said Dora. "*Will he?*"

Ivy's spine tightened under the starched white blouse, then made itself very straight. She slapped down the tea towel and turned to face her.

"What do *you* think?" It was a scream, frozen and chipped out into words. Her eyes glittered like sun on ice. "Eh? *Eh?*" Her voice rose, splintering, the eyes strafing Dora with accusations. "You know what it's been doing, don't you? That filthy animal? Well, do you or don't you? Answer me!"

"NO!" Dora shook her head desperately.

Ivy spat out the words as if they had been soaked in pus.

"Then I'll tell you. Molesting sheep, that's what."

Dora's stomach clenched. "I don't believe it."

"I don't care what you believe. It's time you came out of your dream world, Missy." Ivy's face was contorted with fury. "Do you have any idea what this could cost your father?" She didn't wait for an answer. "They came round here last night, oh, I'm sure you knew all about it, that's why you were creeping round, playing the innocent. They wanted us to hand him over there and then but Fred said No, he'd do it himself."

"Do what?"

Ivy turned away. Picked up a tea towel.

"He broke its neck," she said. And folded the towel. Then again, and again until it was the size of a handkerchief. It wouldn't lie flat. She made her hand into a club and punched it.

"Well, what else could he do?" Pain swerved the woman round to face the girl. Words spewed out of her. "That thing, that *monster*. It should never have been allowed to live in the first place. But try and tell him that! All because he had to please his Baby. All because he goes on and on making promises he can't keep!"

"He kept one, didn't he?" said Dora.

"What choice did he have? It was humane, Dora, believe me. Your father knows how to do these things — A quick twist — it breaks the neck immediately — it wouldn't have felt anything."

She gasped as someone lifted and dropped the door knocker.

"Oh, NO! Mrs Eland — the meeting . . . Dora, I have to go." Reprieved, she was scurrying about, grabbing her coat, throwing it over her shoulders instead of putting it on — something she never did — jamming on her hat, trying to force in the hat-pin.

"Coming!" she called gaily, then to Dora, quickly and urgently: "You won't be too hard on your father, will you?"

And she was gone.

He came in late. Went across to the shallow stone sink in the scullery and washed his hands. Perhaps he took a little longer than usual, perhaps it was her imagination. When he had finished, he came over and took his seat at the table, hauling the loaf towards him in one of those big hands. Killer's hands . . .

She watched him. Rocked herself silently back and forth in Ivy's chair, and watched him.

He picked up the knife. Put it down again.

"Well, what are you staring at?"

"Nothing," she said. And meant it.

He turned to her imploringly. She gave him a small, prim smile. He knew then that words were hopeless, but that he would have to try, say something, anything, that was The Rule. Only he wasn't in charge of The Game any more. His mouth opened.

"What did you do with him after you killed him?" she enquired conversationally. His face went grey. "I'd be interested to know — if it isn't too much trouble."

The face struggled. Words, excuses, trying to punch their way out from under a grey, rumpled blanket. When the voice finally emerged, it was barely audible.

"I thr —"

"Yes?" she prompted, the polite, hostess smile hardening at the edges. He looked at his hands. Then at the tablecloth. Sighed. The voice was flat and empty now. Defeated.

"I threw him in the river," he said.

Oh, God. Dumped, like rubbish. *I hope he bit* you, she thought, *I hope he hurt* you . . . Or maybe he didn't struggle. What was it Ivy said? He wouldn't have felt anything. A quick twist, your father knows how to do these things . . . Did he go along, trusting, thinking it was a new game? Did he lick those hands gratefully as they reached to choke the life out of him? Or perhaps he knew. And licked them anyway . . .

Her father's face had gone out of focus. To her horror, she felt something wet splash on to the back of her hand. She covered it quickly with the other one. But he had seen the tear, and with it his chance of a reprieve. He was getting to his feet, lumbering over, putting out his arms . . .

"*Don't touch me!*" The burst of passion cleared her again, stopping him in his tracks.

Coldly, she observed the big man, rooted in front of her like a tree riven by lightning, his arms sticking out stupidly, his eyes clouded with hurt. She must keep him like that, keep him away from her, because if she once let him near her, near enough to touch, she would break down completely, and that's what he wanted. To hold her fast in his arms while she raged and fought, until all the agony was out in the open for him to see and reckon with instead of hugged tight inside, keeping her closed up and safe from him as she was now. And when the fury was over, she would cling to him for comfort, weeping and calling his name, because there was no one else, cling to him weeping and forgive him and love him again. He was counting on that.

He made a tiny movement towards her and the words flew out, arrows of ice: "Don't come near me! I don't want your comfort! I hate you! You killed Van Gogh! Don't you ever touch me again!"

He put up his hands as if to ward her off, but she drove on relentlessly:

"He never asked to live in the first place. You made him. And then you killed him because he didn't turn out the way you wanted. How could he? You should have known that. *You* never change, in spite of all your promises. You're worse than Ivy, at least she tells the truth!"

The tears were coming again now, but she blazed through them: "You killed Van Gogh because he was ugly. Well what about you?" She turned the sob into a laugh. "You're uglier than he was! Ugly, ugly, ugly, UGLY!"

He had broken through in spite of her. Had hold of her in those hands. She battered at him with her fists, her tears, her words, anything.

"It should have been you that died. Not Mum. Not Van Gogh. It should have been YOU ! You take people's lives, and you spoil them. I wish you were dead. I wish you'd died instead of Mum. I wish you'd die *now* !"

She felt the shock go right through him. Then the flat of his palm, snapping off the stream of words. She gasped, momentarily emptied of rage, adrift. Then found her anchor again. Swung her face back and laughed. Laughed right up at him with the tears bouncing down her cheeks like droplets hissing on a stove.

"Dora! DORA!" He had hold of both wrists now in one huge paw. "Listen to me!"

She whipped her head from side to side, tears flying to left and right. 'Stop it, Dora! Stop it! And look at me! *Look at me*! It's *me*! Your DAD!"

She looked at him, and his world stopped. He saw the mark of his hand on her cheek like a brand, and the hate, glittering and hard as diamonds, and he knew then that there was no hope. But the stupid part of him, the part that she had used to love, told him to keep on trying. I'm just an ordinary bloke, his eyes pleaded. Pity me.

She stared back, unwavering. And in his fear, he became stupider, telling himself that this was his chance, that she wanted him to win, that if he could only make her laugh, it would all be over and everything would be the same as it used to be.

He looked into her eyes. Very, very slowly, he lifted one eyebrow. And waggled it. She stared straight back. He lifted the other. And waggled both. The hatred in her eyes deepened to disgust. He saw himself reflected, a grotesque and pitiful clown, and he knew he should stop it there. But he had no shame left. Summoning all his courage, he rolled his right eye in towards his nose as if he were trying to look at the left one. Her face blurred, but the contempt in it didn't falter. Then he rolled his left eye in to look at the right one, and completed his mask of degredation. Everything went fuzzy, and he felt sick, as if he must fall.

But still the laughter did not come. As she swam back into focus, he searched for a gleam of hope, a quiver of recognition. And the look in her eyes turned his guts to butter.

It was over. He held that look for a second only, then dropped his head. Dora got up slowly and walked out of the room. He heard her feet on the stairs and the flap, flap of her nightgown as it followed her up. The rocking chair swayed back and forth, back and forth. And was still.

CHAPTER 6

Dora stayed in bed as late as she dared, to be quite sure he had gone out. As she came downstairs, something about the cottage struck her as different from usual. It was a moment before she realized what it was — no smell of breakfast cooking. Ivy was sitting at the table. There were no cups on it, no plates, no cutlery. Just a single sheet of paper. As Dora approached, she stood up and handed it to her without a word. It said:

"Gone to join the army. Maybe I can do some good there. Not much use to anyone here. Take care of the girls. Love, Fred."

Dora read it three times. And all she could think was: He didn't leave any message, he wrote to *her*, not me.

"Well, you've got what you wanted now, haven't you?" said Ivy. And her voice was razor blades and stinging nettles.

Dora stared at her. "I don't know what you mean."

"Don't lie to me, you spiteful little cat!" It was like acid in the face. "D'you think I didn't see right through you from the word Go? It was written all over you at the wedding — You were dying, absolutely dying — of *jealousy*!"

Dora stammered a protest, but Ivy cut her off. "Why don't you admit it? You couldn't bear to think of your precious father getting close to anyone else, could you? Well, you've driven us apart now, even if it isn't quite the way you planned it. I suppose you think I'm going to pack my bags and he'll come running back?"

"Ivy, this isn't true, any of it — "

"Well, let me tell you, nothing would give me greater pleasure than to leave the pack of you to each other — You've never made me feel welcome, always treated me as if I were a nasty Headmistress and that Higdon woman was your real mother. But I took you on and I made the best of it. And I've got to go on making the best of it—" She snatched up the letter and thrust it under Dora's nose like a dog mess on a shovel. "Because he expects me to. Even when he's not here, he expects me to do his dirty business for him."

"I'll tell him you said that!" screamed Dora. "You wait!"

"No, missy, *you* wait. Wait and see if he ever comes back." She grabbed Dora by the shoulders and shook her. "It isn't a school outing he's gone on, you stupid little ninny. It's a war! So if he never comes back, just remember, it'll be *your fault!*"

She let go suddenly and sat down, winded by grief, tears studding her cheeks as if they had been hammered full of nails. Dora put her fists to her mouth to jam back the sobs, and lurched from the room.

"You love him now, don't you?" Ivy shrilled after her. "Now you've sent him off to be maimed or gassed or worse! Well, he was laughing at you all the time. You and your stupid Van Gogh!"

"What do you mean?" Dora stopped halfway up the stairs, her knee on one step, hands clutching the one above. She looked down and saw Ivy's face below her, as white and sharp as creased paper.

"Thought it was such a clever name, didn't you? And it was! I'll tell you about Van Gogh—the real one. He was *mad*! Barking *mad*!" Ivy bit back a laugh edged with hysteria. "He only had one ear! He cut the other one off and sent it to a friend through the post! *That's* what your father was thinking of, that's how much he loved your stupid animal!"

Bunched over in agony, Dora hobbled along the passage, bumping off the walls, and fell on to the bed. Even when there were no tears left, the sobs kept coming in dry spasms like sickness when there's nothing left to sick up. When at last they stopped, she lay, face down, hatred buzzing along all her veins, a swarm of stingers let loose inside her head. Then she sat up slowly, and pulled open the drawer of the little table.

It was still wrapped up in its newspaper. The filigree

horse from the market stall. She uncovered it carefully as she did each night before going to sleep. Even now its beauty and fragility enthralled her. She held it up to the light, marvelling at the delicate strength of its curved neck, at the impatient, dancing hooves, eager to be off and cantering on the air. She lowered it to her lap. Tears sprang again into her eyes as she ran a wondering finger over each of the slender glass spun legs. Then, very deliberately, one by one, she snapped them off.

Alex was bored. The new teachers were very nice, but boring. Her new reading book was boring. After break would be boring sums. Boring needlework in the afternoon. And they never *discussed* things any more. They were just told them.

The sound of the door opening woke her from her doze. It was Dora. Instead of apologizing for being late, she strode right up and grabbed her by the arm.

"Come on, Alexandra — We're going over to the *real* school."

The strikers gave them a rapturous welcome.

"We knew your Auntie Ivy would see reason!" said Emily. "My Dad says she's not really toffee nosed, just afraid of Eland."

"And she only got in with him," added Violet, "because they were all new in Burston together, and she was a bit scared of our Mums because they'd all known and loved your real Mum so much."

Alex basked in their approval. Life was good: she was one of the gang again, the dog (so Dora told her) had run off at last, and Dad had gone to be a soldier like other people's dads.

Dora went and sat by herself.

Ivy was shredding suet for dumplings when they came in. They'd had half a bullock's head at the weekend and she'd boiled up a meaty soup from the remains. Watching her work, Dora suddenly recognized what a good housekeeper she was. She'd need to be now, without Dad's money coming in. Maybe they'd end up moving in with Auntie Win if he never . . . She took a deep breath.

"You don't need to tell me," said Ivy. "Mrs Eland gave me the glad tidings. And you may do as you please." She shaped another dumpling between expert fingers and dropped it into the pan. "All I ask is that we try to put up with each other till all this business is over."

Dora went upstairs. Ivy had tidied up, smoothed the coverlet on the bed, straightened the books and pens on the table . . . And the drawer of the table was *shut*. Dora didn't remember shutting it completely. A horrible pang of fear sliced through her. She opened it. The five pieces of broken glass had gone. She stared at the emptiness for a long time, sick with shame at what she had done. Then she went downstairs for supper. The glass horse was never mentioned again.

PART 4: COMING TO TERMS

When wilt thou save thy people,
O, God of Mercy, when?
Thy people, Lord, the people,
Not thrones and crowns, but men.
Flowers of Thy heart and good are they,
Let them not pass like weeds away,
Their heritage a sunless day,
God save the people.

Chapel hymn

CHAPTER I

"Class dismissed! Dora, would you stay behind for a moment?"

Mrs Higdon waited until the last child had disappeared down the ladder from the carpenter's shop, then said: "Is there anything wrong? Your attitude seems to have changed since you came back. You don't take part in things any more. And you've stopped keeping your diary. Why's that?"

Dora shrugged. "What's the point? Emily's writing a book about the Strike."

"You're not jealous, surely? Her success should inspire you."

"To be special? But I'm not, am I? It was all just a trick."

Annie ran a hand over her besom of grey hair.

"You have a gift, Dora. It may have taken a bit of trickery to bring it out, but was I to let you throw yourself away? *All* of the children here have something special, and it's my job to find it. But they have to give something back. Right now, they're all trying their hardest to make the most of themselves — and that's the best kind of support they can give me. Just turning up here isn't worth anything if you do it half heartedly. Or . . . " She looked very hard at Dora. "Or just to spite somebody else."

Dora said nothing. Mrs Higdon picked up her bag. "I'm taking a group of senior girls out tonight to a talk on *Pilgrim's Progress*. Will you come with us?"

"All right, then." At least it'll get me out of the house, she thought.

It was funny: after a telling-off like that she ought to have felt dreadful. But nowadays, when terrible things happened, they didn't seem terrible at all. They seemed unimportant, distant, as if they were happening to somebody else.

I'm growing up, that's what it is, she decided. I'm too old now for writing silly stories or feeling emotional about things. After all, isn't that just what had happened to Dad? He'd married Ivy because he'd finally decided to grow up and do the Right Thing. And he'd given up wanting to be special. Mrs Higdon would call it being half-hearted because it made him stop painting. It had made him stop *feeling* too — wasn't that why he'd walked away?

Well, I can walk away too, Dora told herself. I can slam doors and keep the pain outside. It's good to be grown up.

They set off at six for a chapel two miles away. It was a rosy autumn evening, smelling of bonfires and elderberries, and the leaves were as yellow as potato crisps. Mrs Higdon was in excellent spirits, scudding along like a small and comfortable cloud and waving her arms to draw their attention to the splendours of the countryside.

She looks ridiculous, thought Dora, what on earth does any of it matter?

By now they were skirting the grounds of Burston Hall, a particularly splendid example of rural wealth, owned by a squire who spent most of his time in London. Through the grainy dusk they could see a number of men in grey overalls busily trimming its massive hedges. The tallest of them, who seemed to be in charge, was standing with his back to Mrs Higdon and her party, shouting encouragement at the others. As they approached, he turned and Dora saw him clearly. She gave a sharp involuntary cry.

It was Dad.

The same big, strong frame. The same thick fair hair. The easy, unassuming smile. What was he *doing* here with these strange men? Why didn't anybody know that he hadn't gone to war at all? And why hadn't they *told* her?

Even as she thought these things, the man changed before her eyes, like a lantern slide coming into focus, became quite obviously *not* Dad, taller and thinner, holding himself differently, very erect and formal. She was amazed that she could have been so wrong. But as they drew nearer, she still seemed to see the idea of Dad superimposed on the stranger—like a tracing on greaseproof paper that's been joggled so it doesn't quite match the image underneath. She realized that Violet had taken hold of her hand. She shook it off.

"Wait here a moment, will you, girls?" Mrs Higdon went over to the man, who clicked his heels and gave her a short, respectful bow from the waist. "*Guten abend*," she said. The man smiled broadly and they started talking. The girls looked on, scandalized and delighted. They couldn't understand a word.

"Who *are* they?" whispered Emily.

"German Prisoners," Violet whispered back. "They're doing the work over here that our men can't because they're all over there."

Marjory was shocked.

"D'you think she *ought* to be talking to him?" she sizzled into Violet's ear. "After all, they are The Enemy."

"Oh, Governess knows best," said Violet loftily. "She doesn't believe in war anyway."

Just then Mrs Higdon broke off her conversation and beckoned to Dora. Dora went numb. Violet nudged her.

"Go *on*. You mustn't be rude." Dora moved forward on legs made of sponge.

"This is Captain Meyer," said Mrs Higdon. "He doesn't speak any English, but he has a little French, and I know yours is quite good. Try, Good Evening, Captain Meyer."

"*Bonsoir, Capitaine Meyer.*" The syllables filled up her mouth like mucous, but she managed to push them out. They had an electrifying effect on the Captain: he looked delighted, proud and sad all at the same time, smiling at the Headmistress and looking back at Dora with something terrifyingly like affection.

At a loss, she thrust out her hand for him to shake. This seemed to please him inordinately. He took it in his own, clicked his heels, and gave her a little bow just as he had given Mrs Higdon.

"*Enchanté, Mademoiselle,*" he said.

As he bent over the hand, still inkstained and grubby

from the day's lessons, he lifted it up and brushed it very gently with his lips. She felt the hairs of his moustache prickle the back of her knuckles, and every nerve in her body flared as if probed by a cat's whisker. Before she could snatch it away, he released her and stood to attention again, very formal and respectful.

"The Captain has a little girl your age," explained Mrs Higdon gently. "He misses her very much, and his wife at home. He says that none of them wanted to fight us, and they are all hoping, as we are, that it will be settled before Christmas."

Dora realized that all the other men were looking at her. It's my blonde hair, she decided. I remind them of home.

The girls were in hysterics of envy and curiosity when she rejoined them.

"What did he say to you?"

"What did it feel like when he kissed your hand?"

Dora said nothing. When they reached the chapel, she sat in the flickering dark, staring at the illustrations of the Slough of Despond — a sort of spiritual trench, as far as she could make out — and the Giant Despair, while strange and different images slid between her eyes and the faded white screen. She was wondering if some young German girl in a distant village was reminding Fred Watson of home . . .

And the idea scorched her all over with jealousy.

Next morning a mist came down like a cold wet flannel and the sodden bonfires smelled like sour underwear. As Dora dragged towards school she saw Mrs Higdon, Violet, and old Ambrose deep in conversation.

"I wish you'd reconsider," the Headmistress was saying agitatedly. "We'll do everything we can to help."

"I know," apologized the old man, "but I'm too old for fighting and carrying on. You're a survivor, Governess. You'll win in the end because you don't know how to lose." He turned away, sighing heavily, and they heard his stick tap-tapping through the mist.

"Come on up," said Mrs Higdon. "We've a lot to discuss."

When school was assembled, she told everyone that Ambrose had decided to sell up and leave Burston. It meant that at some time soon, they would have to move out of the shop.

"Don't be downhearted," she said. "We now have a new goal — To buy a plot of land and build our own school!"

Their own school! Where no one could threaten them. A Hall of Freedom — that's what Violet said it would be. But how would they raise the money? They began writing letters to likely supporters, and for everyone but Dora, the time simply flew past.

At dinner-time, Mrs Ling shouted up the ladder: "Marjory — I've brought your bike! Fetch the doctor from Diss — Quick!"

"Mercy! My sister's baby! It's coming at last!"

But the baby did not arrive until the following afternoon. And it was dead when it came.

"Too big," said the Doctor briefly, washing his hands at the sink. "A beautiful boy, too. Pity."

They made a coffin from a shoebox, and lined it with white satin. Before they closed the lid, Marjory peeped inside. He was quite perfect, not a mark on him. She heard her sister weeping upstairs. All that effort for nothing.

"What are we to do?" asked her father. "Eland won't conduct a funeral. He won't even baptize it."

"We'll do both ourselves then!" said his wife. "On the Green — right under his evil eye!"

"But the boy's still got to be buried..."

"Eland can't refuse to let him in the churchyard, can he?"

"I don't know." Ling looked black. "What about *William*?"

"He's Sexton. He'll *have* to bury him. Ask him, dear."

"And give him the chance to refuse? I'd bury myself first!"

"Harry, please! He's your brother!"

"No. Things are too far gone for this to mend them."

"Well, then," said Marjory, "you'd better leave it to me."

That night she crept out of the house with Sabina

Durbidge, carrying the box and a garden spade. They made their way to the north side of the churchyard which couldn't be seen from the road, dug a small hole under a yew tree and placed the shoebox inside. Terrified of being spotted, for several cottages overlooked the churchyard, they whispered a short prayer and patted the earth flat to make it look normal. Then they ran home as fast as their wobbling legs would allow them.

But somebody had seen. Dropping the white lace curtain with its pattern of swans, Ivy turned sadly back into her bedroom. And ran her hands over her belly as if fearful that something might try to threaten the new life inside it.

CHAPTER 2

Christmas came again. Ivy and the girls spent the holiday with Auntie Win, but things could have been worse — At least they didn't have to go to the Rector's on Boxing Day, as they did usually. Ivy said Auntie Win was too delicate to be left, which wasn't surprising as she'd managed to devour three slices of plum pudding and half a decanter of port during the Christmas meal.

"Aren't you going to go to church any more?" asked Alex, suspecting that there was more to it.

Ivy skinned her with a look. "Of course I will!" She still felt she owed the Elands a debt of friendship, but she had changed her pew (there was plenty of choice now) and no longer sat by the North door. Sometimes her eyes strayed to the window on the far side and the dark yews nodding outside and she would turn away, covering her face . . .

At last the festivities were over and they set off home in the trap. A heavy snow had fallen and crisped over, munching up the sound of the pony's hooves. As they entered Burston, they saw Henry Garnham walking ahead of them. In spite of the cold, he had taken off his billycock hat, and they noticed for the first time that his hair had turned white to match that obstinate thrust of beard.

"Happy New Year, Mr Garnham!" they chorused.

He didn't even see them. In his ungloved hand he was holding a letter crunched up like a frozen leaf. It was from the War Office. His son Herbert, who had sung so beautifully at the carol concert one Christmas Eve ages ago, had been killed in action.

When school reopened next day, everyone was in low spirits. The war on their own doorstep had tended to make them forget what was happening abroad. Herbert's death brought it closer.

Mrs Higdon read them some poems written by soldiers in the trenches. Some were stirring and patriotic, others full of despair and suffering, of ruptured lungs coughed up into clouds of poisoned gas. Many of the children wept to hear them.

Dora sat unmoved. Nothing could touch her now. She had withdrawn so far from hurt, it was like being underwater. Guilt, anger, pain, were all bullets crawling after her too slowly ever to catch up.

"I'd like you to try and write some poetry yourselves," said Mrs Higdon. "It will help you to understand your own feelings."

Dora had no intention of writing anything, but as soon as she picked up her pen, the bullets speeded up, firing ideas into her head. Ideas she didn't like, but felt somehow impelled to get right.

"A burst of shell fire left him blind, And howling in the mud and rain . . . " She scrawled it out. Melodramatic rubbish! Then a whole verse appeared in front of her eyes, and she simply copied it down.

Mrs Higdon gathered up the poems and started to read them during the dinner hour. She called out of the window to Dora who was wandering aimlessly round the Green. As the child's feet creaked reluctantly up the ladder, Annie read the verse again.

> She sat up suddenly in bed
> And reached a hand out in the dark
> Regretting things that she had said
> And things she had not said. A spark
> Of moonlight lit the frosty pane
> Then all was dark again.
> Dark was the room and dark the bed
> Darkest of all inside her head
> Yet still the white hand reached in vain
> Knowing for certain he was dead.

"It's about your father, isn't it?" said Annie putting her hand on the girl's shoulder.

Dora moved away, lips tight. "Stop pretending that you can't feel," persisted the teacher. "This poem proves that you do. You're facing the pain, and it's brought your gift back."

"If that's a gift, I don't want it."

"Wouldn't it help you to talk about things?"

"What is there to say? I've killed my father. What d'you want me to do? Scream and shout? Like a little baby? I wish I'd never written the bloody thing—" She snatched the paper and ripped it into a whirl of shreds. " *There!*"

Mrs Higdon's face trembled.

"You can't tear up feelings . . . Isn't that what this strike is all about?"

Dora turned her back.

"You don't know that he is dead," went on the teacher. "You do know that he would be glad you've started working again."

"Why should he care? If he'd cared, he wouldn't have gone away." But isn't that *why* he went, said a secret voice — because he cared so much he couldn't stand it? She flicked her head and the bullet grazed her cheek.

"He will care now, wherever he is," said Mrs Higdon.

Dora had a sudden vision of the German officer and the sadness in his eyes when he talked about his little girl. She flailed round at the Headmistress.

"Why don't you mind your own business and leave me alone!"

She did not return for afternoon lessons.

Everyone else got busy with preparations for what was to be the biggest meeting yet. Two hundred members from nine branches of the Railwaymen's Union were coming to Burston on their own special train. The children worked tirelessly making banners for the procession and printing leaflets advertising the occasion:

> **A VILLAGE IN REVOLT!**
> **A FIGHT FOR FREEDOM AND JUSTICE!**
> Come and hear for yourselves how Mr and Mrs Higdon and the brave women of Burston have, since April, 1914, nobly struggled against the tyranny of the PARSON & Landowners.

The classroom was scoured. Mabel polished up the brown wooden desks as if they were racehorses, window panes sparkled, the burnished pipe above the stove glowed like the bronze throat of an eastern princess. Jimmy Wittle even offered to wash the floor!

"You can come and do ours afterwards, if you like!" said Tom, only half joking. Violet started typing out a book he had written about the strike which he was hoping to publish, and Emily rehearsed readings from her own account which had received a definite offer from Lusher Brothers of Diss.

"It's much more fun having a war at home," declared Sabina. "At least nobody dies!" Everyone but Marjory thought this was hilarious.

Later on, they changed their minds.

The snow squeaked under Dora's boots as she crossed Crown Common and started walking away from the village. Above her, the patient trees carried their white burdens like armfuls of freshly folded bedlinen. Misery clung to her like wet leaves. She lifted her face and trudged on.

Someone was walking ahead of her, a weary ghost, white haired and thin, like an image of her own pain. Has he been walking all night? she wondered. Does his wife know where he is? In spite of herself, she started hurrying to catch him up.

"Mr Garnham! *Mr Garnham!*"

He stopped by the Philpot cottage and turned slowly. And Dora saw the face of a dead man. As empty as if it had been eaten away from the inside by ants. The eyes struggled to recognize her.

She had nothing prepared. What could she say except all the things he was walking away from the village to escape? What could she offer but the sympathy *she* was running away from too, because sympathy made you start feeling again.

"Shouldn't you go home, Mr Garnham?" she said. "Your wife will be worried about you."

He stood there, shivering, his eyes moving vaguely over her face. Snow started to fall. Tentatively, she took him by the arm. The sleeve of his jacket was cold and stiff — his clothes had congealed around him like grave cloths, brittle with frost.

"Come along, Mr Garnham," she said. "Let me take you home."

She gave him a gentle tug and he started walking again, his feet slurring through the snow. As they passed the Old Mill where the Higdons now lived, he seemed to recollect himself.

"You're very kind," he said, and his voice was the voice of an old man, terribly tired and sad. "Just like your father."

You mean like he *was*, she thought. But she couldn't say that. Her own fears seemed selfish compared with real grief.

"I'll always be grateful to him," went on Garnham, "for helping me out with the harvest that time."

He was rambling of course, but what harm to let him go on? She knew what he was talking about. It was just before Dad left. The whole village had turned out by moonlight to help Garnham get in his crops because Eland wouldn't let him on to his Glebe during the day. But Dad wasn't involved. No one was speaking to him.

"Of course we swore not to tell," Garnham was saying. "But what does it matter now?"

And then she saw it all. Dad tramping home from a distant farm, seeing the people gathered to help out a friend. Cat-calls as he went past — "Blackleg! Still sending your girls to the Council School?" And Dad making a joke or two back and then a decision: "Give us that scythe!"

Gripping it in his blistered hands. "But don't tell the wife!"

Typical. Trying to please everybody at the same time. Suddenly it didn't seem such a crime. Suddenly it seemed terribly touching, almost noble. It wasn't half-hearted at all. It was *whole* hearted...

Garnham must have felt the jolt of pain, for he stopped and looked at her properly for the first time.

"You didn't know?" he said. "I thought Sam Todd—"

"Sam Todd?" Something horrible started to gouge itself into her mind. "You mean he *saw*?"

"Oh, yes. We gave him a penny not to tell his pa, but I expect he did. I wasn't surprised Fred left soon after."

"That's not why he left!" cried Dora. "That wasn't the—"

"Are you all right, child?"

She clutched his arm and started walking again very fast as if trying to catch up with her thoughts. She heard again Sam Todd's howls of dismay as his father clipped him round the ear, then the silence, the whispering and the snort of laughter—"That'll teach him to side with the lame dogs!" She knew now what the words meant, and who it was who had come knocking at their door late that night.

So that's what the Higdons were up against—folks who'd make a man strangle his own dog to pay him back for looking after his friends. No wonder they hated Governess and Master—because the Higdons were whole hearted too, just like Dad. Growing up hadn't made them lose anything, not any of the important things.

"Oh, Dad," she whispered. "What have they done to us?"

Suddenly, there was the school, glowing warm and friendly through the chafing whirl of snowflakes.

"Go in, child," said Garnham gently. "I'll be all right now. D'you know we've just walked all the way round the Candlestick?"

Dora put her foot on the ladder. I'm going to be whole hearted from now on, she told herself. I'm going to stand up for the Higdons to prove I can stand up for Dad. When he comes back, he'll be proud of me. And if he doesn't come back... Well I won't use that as an excuse. I've made too many excuses already.

CHAPTER 3

Goodbye, Little Willie,
Farewell Kaiser Bill,
It's a long long way to Burston Station,
But we're ALL—ON—STRIKE—STILL!

The dark figure at the Rectory window observed the heads of Burston's children bobbing above his hedge like a row of ducks in a shooting gallery, and his eyes narrowed. It was Sunday, and the strikers were off to the station to collect their supporters for the rally. Mrs Eland glanced up from her sewing.

"What are they singing about? It sounds very patriotic."

The Rector gave her a cold look. "For your information," he said, "Kaiser Bill is supposed to be myself, and Little Willie . . ."

"The Sexton, I suppose?"

"Droll, don't you think?"

Actually, she did, though she wasn't foolish enough to say so. She concentrated on her pattern of lazy daisy, and debated whether to favour purple petals or pink. Small wonder Charles was in an even worse mood than usual. There had only been three people in church that morning. Any day now there would be a letter from the Bishop suggesting a move . . . Not that she'd object: Burston was very low society. Even Ivy Watson, so favourably connected with Winifred Wallace (widow of Wally Wallace, the cotton baron) had proved a disappointment. No control over those girls of hers at all . . .

A heavy fist clouted the door, and Eland's face twitched violently. The terrified maid was sent to investigate. But it was only Bob Ford.

"Terrible news about Garnham's boy," wheezed the fat

farmer, wedging himself into a dainty little chair and accepting a cup of tea from Mrs Eland. "Catching a bullet like that. This damn war. And no signs of it ending yet."

"Garnham won't thank you for your sympathy," remarked his host. "When did you last even speak to each other?"

"Oh, he's not so bad," returned Ford. "But whoever would have thought he'd side with those blasted Higdons?"

Mrs Eland clicked her tongue.

"Beg your pardon, ma'am. Those *flaming* Higdons. But the point is, we should bloody well stick together when there's a war on, instead of making war here at home." He emptied the miniature cup in a single gulp. "So I'm thinking of a way we can make up. Herbert was my favourite nephew. What if I was to put up a stone tablet in the church, a sort of monument? To show respect?"

Eland fingered his chin. One thing was certain: the Bishop would be mightily impressed. "An excellent idea, Ford . . . Where there is discord let us sow peace! If we can mend the rift in your own family, it would be an example to others, like the Lings, for example. But tread warily, Bob . . . Don't tell Garnham just yet — he might try to put a spoke in. Let it be a surprise!"

That way, he thought, *we'll* have the edge. We'll be the peacemakers — and they won't *dare* object, it'd look too mean.

Meanwhile the railwaymen were pouring off the train, unfurling their gorgeous silk banners, emerald and silver, purple and crimson, like an army of Christmas trees. From Catford and Colchester they came, from Bury and Beccles, Norwich and Northampton. Led by the pipes and drums of the Bermondsey Railway Band, they strode into Burston, blaring defiance as they passed the Rectory and gathered on the Green where Brother Carter, the organizing secretary, let rip a rousing speech.

"Comrades!" he began. "We're here today to pledge our support to Brother Higdon and his brave supporters, who have struggled so long against oppression and mean mindedness. Their struggle is ours and every working man's, and we'll see them vindicated or there'll be a jolly row! Meantime we must all pull together to see that Burston's dream — its very own Strike School — becomes a reality. A plot of land has been selected and plans drawn up — One thousand pounds, brothers, that's what we need! I propose to hold meetings in Hyde Park and Trafalgar Square, where Comrades Tom and Annie and the children can tell the whole world their story! I'll arrange personally for them to be lodged and entertained handsomely — So three cheers for the Higdons, the children, and the mothers of Burston!"

Next day a mean, stinging rain nibbled away the last of the snow. Inside the carpenter's shop it was lovely and warm, and an assortment of damp cloaks were soon steaming merrily round the stove where chestnuts and potatoes were roasting ready for dinner time. Mrs Higdon was in spanking good spirits. She pinned a map of Burston to the blackboard and pointed out the Village Green.

"This is where we are now," she said. "Down here on the far side. And this is where we're going to be. Exactly opposite.'

"Next to the church!" breathed Violet, awestruck by the daring of it.

"Precisely! We'll build the school on this little plot, facing the Green — with its *back* to the church!"

There were roars of approval. Then a sudden and muffled cry from the back of the room. Mrs Higdon whirled round. Sabina Durbidge was clutching her head, rocking backwards and forwards.

"It hurts, Madam, it *hurts*! Something terrible!"

Mrs Higdon whisked to her side. "Where does it hurt?"

"Everywhere. All down my neck . . ."

"We must get you home at once. Violet, go for the doctor."

Tom carried the girl down the school ladder as carefully as if she were made of tissue paper. She was unconscious by the time he reached the bottom.

Nobody could concentrate after this, so school closed early. Ivy was so alarmed by the news, she actually stopped polishing the lamps and sat down.

"Brain fever," she whispered. "Her poor mother . . . "

Dora was surprised. Ivy had never had time for any of the Durbidges. They fidgeted away the afternoon, unable to settle to anything. At four o'clock, Violet came to the door. They read the news in her face before she could open her mouth.

"Dead?"

"Yes. She never even woke up."

Just then Emily hurried up the path.

"I've brought a note for you, Mrs Watson. From the Parson." Ivy's hand trembled as she unfolded the paper and read the contents. A spasm crossed her face. She crumpled the note and threw it into the stove. Her cheeks were paler than her apron.

"No reply," she told Emily, and bolted out of the room.

"Let's read it!" said Violet, darting over to the stove. Luckily it had gone out. She fished out the paper. "Listen to this: '*Dear Mrs Watson, I have ordered an inquest into the death of the Durbidge girl, which was undoubtedly caused by the appalling conditions of the Strike School. I trust I may count on your support at the hearing.*' Why that's — that's *dastardly*!"

On the day of the inquest, Ivy got up early and started tidying the house from top to bottom. When she had finished, she started again, pausing only when the Coroner's car drove by, and gripping her scrubbing brush so hard it left marks in her hands.

Mrs Durbidge was called three times to answer questions.

"Is it not true," demanded Eland, "that the children had to meet their teachers with no hats on during the wet weather?"

"No, sir. Governess was always particular about them wearing proper clothes. If they didn't have any, she'd lend them some."

"But they do have to cross a common to get to school, which has been either snowbound or waterlogged for months?"

"If their feet got wet, she'd dry their boots out in front of the schoolroom fire."

"Which was never lit until dinner time, I believe."

"It was lit before they got there. You ought to know she kept a good fire, Parson. Wasn't that why you sacked her?"

"I'll thank you not to be impertinent, Madam. This is a serious inquiry."

"Oh, they're all serious inquiries, aren't they?" wept the woman. "And we're the ones that suffer for them afterwards."

Annie Higdon was irate when she found out what was going on.

"Go in there, George, and tell them not to tease your wife any more, or I'll go myself!" Durbidge came out again, shaking and sick with anger. He seemed to have lost stones in minutes.

"They've ordered a post mortem," he said. "They're going to cut up my little girl."

The post mortem confirmed the doctor's original diagnosis. Meningitis. The Strike School was completely absolved.

"It don't help my child, though, does it?" said Durbidge, "that they cut her all to pieces before she could go into the ground."

The Coroner looked shamefaced as he left. "I've attended many inquests in my time," he told Tom Higdon in a low murmur, "but never one like this."

Dora was exhausted when she let herself into the house, which by now was so clean it made her teeth tingle. She walked into the kitchen — and stopped in her tracks.

"I suppose there'll be a Strike Funeral?" asked Ivy.

"Yes," answered Dora. "On the Green." Her voice sounded far away, as if she were speaking to herself on the telephone. She couldn't take her eyes from Ivy's hand — and what she was holding in it. Ivy was saying something in a timid voice:

"D'you think that the Durbidges might consider coming here — afterwards?"

She looked anxiously at Dora, waiting for her approval. Something in Dora recognized that she had made a huge leap forward, but she could not answer, just kept her eyes fixed on the wispy lump of hair between Ivy's fingers. There were grey strands in it — funny how she had never noticed them before.

"What are you looking at?" asked Ivy. "Oh — *this*! I found it shoved away in the back of a drawer. I don't know *what* Alexandra can have been thinking of."

"Alexandra?" said Dora faintly.

"I suppose it proves one thing," Ivy went on. "She obviously *did* brush that poor animal, though you'd never have known. Ugh!" Her face squirmed with distaste. "Fancy keeping it! Still, only one thing to do with it now." She picked up the poker and lifted the lid of the stove. This time it was lit.

"WAIT!"

She stopped, just too late. There was a faint sizzling sound, and the smell of scorched hair writhed up in a twist of blue smoke. Then Ivy realized. Her hands flew to her mouth and her eyes above them went pale with horror. She mumbled something into her fingers, then crumpled up into her chair and started weeping as if she were being whipped. Horror-struck, Dora stood helpless as the black plaits fell down over the woman's face.

"Don't cry — You didn't know. *Please* — I can't bear it."

"I'm so sorry, Dora," wept Ivy. "Forgive me . . ."

"Forgive you!" Dora knelt down and tried to get through the tangle of fingers and tears and hair. "I should be asking you to forgive *me*!"

Ivy shook her head, riven with remorse. "I've spoiled everything. I'll go away . . ."

"No!" Dora clutched Ivy's hands and pulled them away from her face. "Don't let me drive *you* away too!"

"I didn't want to replace your mother," sobbed Ivy. "And I didn't ask him to take down her pictures. But when he did, I thought he wanted a new start. And I was so scared of doing the wrong thing . . . "

How young she looks, thought Dora, terribly young. After all, she can't have been much more than a child herself when she married Dad. Trying too hard. Afraid to be soft.

"Wait a minute." She got up and took the old silver-backed brush from the drawer. Very gently she began to brush out the long hair, and Ivy grew calmer, like a child being rocked. "I wasn't fair," said Dora. "I know Mum would've wanted you here. She said once you were like the little sister she never had, but I didn't want to remember that — because *I* wanted to take her place. I think I've been on a sort of strike of my own for a long time, and not the right kind. Have you been terribly lonely?"

Mercifully Ivy didn't reply. "I'm sure Mrs Durbidge would be glad to come here," went on Dora, "if you're well enough?"

Ivy stiffened. "Why shouldn't I be?"

"Well, you've been sick an awful lot lately. I've heard you in the mornings. You're not ill, are you?"

And then, all in a rush, she understood. The brush clattered to the floor. "*Ivy!* You're not — I mean, *are* you?"

"Oh, Dora — You won't mind too much, will you?"

"*Mind?* It's the most wonderful thing I ever heard!"

"D'you honestly mean that?" Ivy jumped up. "Come on then! Let's get all the pictures down from the attic and make this a *real* home again!"

CHAPTER 4

After the funeral, Durbidge enlisted and went off to fight. Bob Ford's tribute to Herbert Garnham now became a matter of urgency. One day in spring, the fat farmer beckoned Violet into the church, grunting: "Come and see! You'll be sorry you didn't!"

Two minutes later, she was pelting over to Henry Garnham's.

"It's a WHAT?"

"A stone tablet. On the wall of the nave. In Memory of Herbert Garnham, killed in action in France, erected by his uncle R.B. Ford..."

The following Sunday, Eland and Ford were delighted to see Henry Garnham, pale and thin, but straight-backed inside his best three-piece suit, arrive for morning worship with his wife and daughter Daisy. They filed meekly into their pew—immediately below the stone tablet. Sunlight streamed through the stained glass figures of Mary and her Blessed Babe, streaking with red the slab of white marble. Eland mounted the pulpit and lifted his reedy tenor to praise The Prince of Peace. The Sexton added his baritone and Ford his rumbling bass, and the organ crunched out its golden chords. The Garnhams stood silent.

Suddenly, as if he were vaulting over a gate, Garnham put a hand on the back of the pew and sprang up on to it, thrusting his face so close to the tablet, the tip of his white beard grazed the inscription. He paused for a moment, with his other hand inside his jacket, staring at the words. Then he took a step back, and his arm swung out, his fist clubbing a great black coalhammer. Up went the arm— and round—and down. It smacked through the stone tablet with a sound like graves opening and a huge ragged crack opened up in it from top to bottom.

"Swine!" screamed Garnham. "Swine! Swine! *Swine!*"

His arm swung round again, and marble chips flew out from the surface, scattering Ford's apology all round the nave.

Time stopped. The singing stopped. But the organist played on, oblivious. Garnham paused, gathering his strength like a reaper readying himself for the final row, then flung the hammer up for a third time. With a cry, Eland leaped from the pulpit and threw himself on the man's legs. Mrs Garnham battered him with her hymn-book, the Sexton scrambled over the intervening pews, and the hammer flailed wildly as the scuffle spilled out into the aisle.

White to the chops with fury, Ford plunged out of the church. Daisy aimed a thump at him and missed, smacking Eland in the back so hard the air squeaked out of his chest as if he'd been sat on.

"Oink! Oink!" she raged at the retreating farmer. "Back to your trough, you ugly old pig!" Ling hurled her to the floor, blacking her eye, and they were hustled like convicts from the holy place. The organ thundered on.

A little later, the Sexton slipped out of the north door and sidled through the nettles, eager to get home to his roast beef. His gleaming black shoes, newly heeled at great expense in Diss, (he was boycotting his brother's business) squelched in the wet earth. He lifted his foot, tutting, then froze — at the sound of another squelch behind him. Turning, he saw Tom Higdon standing among the tombstones — and *smiling*. The Sexton's legs turned as soft as sticks of boiled rhubarb. He hurled himself forwards, grabbing at yew branches while the mud sucked and gripped his shiny feet — heard Tom's booming laugh and the sound of easy, determined strides. The next thing he knew, he was airborne and flying towards the church gate like a battering ram.

"This is for the good conduct you showed Daisy this morning!" roared Higdon.

"For pity's sake!" squealed the Sexton. "I'll be sick!"

Tom dropped him by the gate and ran off, jeering like a schoolboy. Not a dignified affair.

Garnham got a month's hard labour. Higdon was fined a pound. Daisy was bound over to keep the peace. The entire family burst into tears in the courtroom. So much for peaceful overtures.

"When does it stop, Violet?" asked Dora, as they cycled back from court together. "All this bitterness, all this hate?"

"It'll stop when we've won!"

"But doesn't there come a point—even when you *know* you're right—when being whole-hearted just means being obstinate?"

"We've gone too far to stop," said Violet. "It's like the war. If we back down now, things will be worse than before. They'll never give us another chance to fight for our freedom. And people who come after us will be afraid to try. So we just *have* to win."

"We *are* winning!" crowed Mrs Higdon, bicycling up behind them. "Stop a minute, I'm out of puff, and I've something to tell you." They stopped. "Eland's *leaving Burston*!"

"He's *what*?" Violet hurled her hat in the air and sent a whoop after it. "You see, Dora! You see! It was all worth it!"

"This is the best bit," giggled Mrs Higdon. "He's being moved to a sphere *more genial*—Sawtrey, near Cambridge. It's *tiny*! He can't do much damage there! Now, listen. I'm making a list of everyone who's helped with the strike. When we get our own school, I'll put up a plaque inside with your names on. There you'll be in letters of gold—Violet Potter and Dora Watson!"

"You can't put *my* name! I didn't join till the last minute."

"But you *did* join, Dora. You stood up and were counted. That's worth knowing about yourself. You've never had to pretend you were somebody by frightening the innocent and the weak. So don't think I approve of everything that's come out of this strike. It saddens me that a crisis always brings out the bad as well as the good. Think about it, anyway, promise me that."

One evening in early spring as the light faded on the picture of Dora's mum which now hung over the mantlepiece in the front parlour, Ivy put aside her sewing and said calmly, "I think you'd better fetch the midwife, Dora."

"What? You mean the baby — ?"

"Yes, dear." Unexpected pain seared the woman's face and her lips whitened. She caught Dora's arm. "You'd better hurry!"

"But she isn't here!" gabbled Dora, panicking. "None of the women are here! They've all gone to a Labour meeting!"

"A Labour meeting! How appropriate!" Ivy started to laugh which turned into a gasp. Her fingers gnawed into Dora's arm. Dora gazed at her in terror.

"What shall I do? Shall I cycle to Diss for the Doctor?"

"No time! You'll have to be like Mrs Higdon and improvise!"

In a room overlooking the sea — the first sea she had ever seen in her life, Violet woke up with a shriek.

"What was that noise?"

Everyone sat up in bed. Above the soft explosions of surf they heard the sickening boom of a real explosion, and a violent light turned all their faces into magic lantern slides. Mrs Higdon stumbled to the window and let out a squawk as her toe struck a cold porcelain object that felt like a landmine. She clawed back the curtain.

"A German Zeppelin!" she cried. "Oh, you should see it, girls! It's as big and fat and full of wind as old Bob Ford!"

There was another bang and the room rattled round them like a mouthful of loose teeth. Everyone dived under the blankets and prayed like mad. Mrs Higdon got down on her knees, wincing at a rheumatic twinge, then sprang up again with a cry of disgust.

"What *nincompoop* knocked over the chamber pot?"

Under the blankets, while the bombs fell outside, muffled detonations of laughter went off all around the room.

"Look, Ivy! Look, Alex! It's a little boy!"

Ivy covered her face.

"I daren't," she murmured. "Is he — Is he . . .?"

"He's perfectly fine! And *hungry* ! Here — take him."

Dora turned away discreetly and stepped outside. Dawn was filling up a wide pale sky. A bird whistled like a bicycle pump. The fields were starting to steam like washing day. She walked up to the gate and leaned on it gratefully, breathing in the smell of apple blossom. A huge yawn engulfed her. She covered her mouth guiltily, glancing round.

And her heart stopped.

The German soldier was walking up the lane towards her. She recognized the build and the fair hair and the uniform. Only the uniform was wrong. It was what the English soldiers would have worn — like Dad. As she watched, the man changed and was yet the same, as if Dad and the soldier had been superimposed on each other. And then he saw her, and started to run — and as he ran, the German soldier was left behind and it *was* Dad! Older, and the hair was mixed with grey, and the sadness in the eyes was like the soldier's had been, but it was *Dad* ! She opened the gate, and the sadness in his eyes changed to hope, and the hope to joy and thankfulness as she ran to meet him.

"With joy and thankfulness I declare this school open to be for ever a hall of freedom!"

Bursting with pride, Violet gazed round at the crowd. The entire village was massed on the Green surrounded by supporters from every part of the country. She led forward a smartly dressed lady. "It is now my great pleasure to introduce our Guest of Honour — Mrs Sylvia Pankhurst, the leader of the Suffragettes!"

Mrs Pankhurst drew off one of her lavender coloured gloves and placed her hand against the wall of the new school. "Brothers and sisters!" she began. "These stones, so lovingly set one on another by the people of Burston, shout out a battle cry — that the human spirit can *never be crushed* !

This school will be a monument not only to the freedom fighters of Burston, but to Freedom itself! The war in Europe continues, my own battle to win votes for women is far from won, but we will keep on fighting! Mrs Higdon has been called an impossible woman. If that be so, then long live *all* impossible women — for they have proved today that we can make the impossible *possible* !"

During the tumult of whistles and applause, a thin, shadowy figure crept out of the north door of the church. Some minutes later a black car glided past the Village Green. The gentleman inside sat motionless, but the lady in the back seat couldn't resist peeking through her veil at the new building.

Small but solid it stood, and as uncompromising as its Headmistress — with its *back* to the church. To the swelling cheers were added the happy shouts of Burston's youngest citizen, Fred Higdon Watson, who, perched on his Dad's shoulders, had come with his mum and sisters, a family at last, to welcome the Higdons to their new school.

TERMINUS

This is a true story of the longest strike in history. Everyone in this book existed, apart from Dora's family, Mabel, Jimmy and Sam. William Ling is really two people put together — the Sexton and the Churchwarden.

In 1989 I visited Burston. Maurice Philpot, a Trustee of the School, (no relation to Mrs Philpot!) let me into the tiny building. It's hard to imagine seventy children in one room, but Annie, true to form, made sure there were plenty of windows for fresh air, and a sturdy fireplace with FREEDOM JUSTICE HUMANITY inscribed above. A plaque lists the children involved, and on the walls outside are the names of those who contributed to the building.

The school flourished until Tom's death on the eve of the Second World War. Annie struggled on, refusing help, and it gradually went into decline, although for seven months of the year it is still technically available as a school. During the other months it functions as museum, lecture hall, exhibition centre, and children's turnpike library.

Tom and Annie are buried side by side in the churchyard. Tom's headstone bears the words IN GOOD WORKS ABUNDANT; Annie's TILL THE DAY BREAK.

P.S.